1

Acknowledgements

There is no way this book could ever have made it to what you are holding in your hands without the many leaders, both good and bad, I have experienced in my life and I want to acknowledge the impact they have had on my life. I am extremely grateful for having had the experience with each one and for what they taught me, not just about leadership, but about who I am!

Along this journey of writing this book I have had a great many people who have been supportive, encouraging and at times real task masters, and I greatly appreciate their efforts. My greatest support and inspiration has been my wife Kay, for whom I will always be grateful that she is in my life and has chosen to stick by me.

I want to thank my niece, Andrea Nelson! Your love, support, encouragement and willingness to be my editor will forever have a special place in my heart. Thank you seems hardly enough for the work you have done to make this book better. Remember, you always have been and always will be my favorite!

And last but not least, I want to dedicate, with great love, this book to my parents, who each struggled their whole life with the baggage of their life and the lessons I learned as a result of their struggles with life.

Table of Contents

Introduction

"Leadership is the art of getting someone else to do something you want done because he wants to do it."

Dwight Eisenhower

CHAPTER ONE

The Leadership Star

"One key notion is the fact that entropy – the dissipation of energy, slow death – operates on both the human ego and the organizational culture. Individuals and organizations are continually pulled toward entropy."
Robert E. Quinn
"Build the Bridge As You Walk On It"

I chose to start off with the above quote because it is indicative of where we are today. Quinn, in his first book, *"Deep Change"* advocates that in order to transform today's organizations leaders must go through a deep change within themselves in order to look at things differently. In a later book, *"Build the Bridge As You Walk On It"* Quinn follows up with the above quote and goes on to say, "Given the choice between deep change and slow death, people tend to choose slow death." Why would that be so? What is so terrifying about deep change? Why would we as individuals, and organizations, prefer to die or go out of existence rather than embracing deep change? For many years, I have been studying, leadership, a subject I find fascinating, and I have come to an understanding about leadership and a conclusion of how leaders can improve to accomplish great things. I agree with Quinn that deep change is a mandatory step, and it is a step that each of us must

"The best executive is the one who has sense enough to pick good men to do what he wants done, and self-restraint to keep from meddling with them while they do it."

Theodore Roosevelt

make within ourselves. In order to be successful in the future, leaders must look within themselves and discover the Truth of who they are, what they want, what they are passionate about and where they want to go. Leaders of tomorrow must embrace change, not only on a deep personal level, but on an organizational level. Change is something that human beings have had to deal with throughout our evolution. Yet, study after study has revealed that we fear change. Why? Again, what are we afraid of? Is it the sense of losing control? Of not knowing where we are going or what will happen? In today's fast-paced world it seems that change is occurring faster than we can keep up. There are those throughout organizations everywhere and in society as well, who want to "go back to the old ways." They want things to remain as they have always been, partly because it is more comfortable. However, the rapidly changing world of today will not allow us to remain the same, let alone go back to the way things were!

Today's leaders have to constantly deal with rapid changes in the marketplace, changes in technology, changes in communication systems and even more importantly, changes in the workforce. Today's workers are smarter, better educated, more savvy and have a driving need to be a part of what is going on in the organization that their predecessors did not seem to have. Leadership in the past was seldom discussed as something separate from 'management.' Only within the past couple of decades has there been a rise in under-

"If you learn just one trick, Scout, you'll get along a lot better with all kinds of folks. You never really understand a person until you consider things from his point of view....until you climb inside his skin and walk around in it."

Atticus Finch
"To Kill a Mockingbird"

standing of the functions of a leader. Today you can find a wide variety of books on leadership focusing on many different aspects of a very complex topic.

One thing that I have come to deeply understand is that Leadership per se cannot be taught separate and apart from the leader and who that leader is, deep inside the heart of who they are. In many leadership classes, and later in this book, I ask the question, "Who are you?" so you might begin thinking about it now. Who are you deep inside? Who are you when you are alone with your own thoughts and no one else is around? Scary, aybe, but definitely necessary!

For over ten years, I taught classes in the MBA program of a rapidly growing private university. Leadership was one subject I taught and the one that often generated the greatest amount of discussions from the students. This university had a large international student population and I was fortunate to have many of these students in my classes. The main thing I found interesting was regardless of culture or country of origin the interest in leadership was strong and there was an almost unanimous opinion that there was more to leadership than the ability to learn competencies. There was a primary focus in the discussions about "who" the leader was, not in name or title, but in nature of who they were inside. Why is this so important today? Is it more important today than in the past? What has caused this yearning to focus on "who" our leaders are as opposed to "what" our leaders have accomplished or can accomplish?

"Leadership is not magnetic personality—that can just as well be a glib tongue. It is not "making friends and influencing people"—that is flattery. Leadership is lifting a person's vision to higher sights, the raising of a person's performance to a higher standard, the building of a personality beyond its normal limitations."

Peter F. Drucker

Over the past couple of decades, our focus on what leadership is, or what makes a leader successful has gone through a dramatic refocusing of what it means to be a leader. In the past, we of course, looked at some of the greatest leaders of the past and looked at what skills they had that made them great leaders, primarily, we seemed to look at their intelligence level and said that intelligence must be a fundamental component of leadership. In the 1990's, Daniel Golman, enlightened and enlivened the study of leadership by positing that it was not mental intelligence (IQ) that made a leader successful, instead it was emotional intelligence (EI). The business world, around the world, became fascinated by the concepts of EI and instituted many programs to determine the EI of their potential leaders. Today, there seems to be a growing interest in another level, or multiple levels of intelligence. The growing focus seems to be on SI – spiritual intelligence. Cindy Wigglesworth, author and organizational consultant in Texas has done a great deal of work in this area and says that even EI is not enough to help leaders survive and thrive. She says that leaders must become more spiritually intelligent. What does this means? It means recognizing the need of workers to be a part of something greater than themselves.

While teaching at the university I taught a variety of courses and the one I taught most often, along with leadership was Organizational Behavior. Over the course of my time at the university we used the same text book in this course, although it was revised many times during my tenure. The last class I taught at the university

"Be gentle and you can be bold; be frugal and you can be liberal; avoid putting yourself before others and you can become a leader among men."

Lao Tzu

was in 2008 and the text for OB was a new revision and had a section that I had never seen in any textbook anywhere and greatly intrigued me: Spirituality in the Workplace. I loved what the text had to say on the subject as it wrote the thoughts I had had on the subject for quite some time. Spirituality is a very interesting word that seems to mean different things to different people. The authors of the text pointed that in this case they were not talking about religious belief, but about a belief in something greater that ourselves, a need to be a part of that something greater. What does this mean in the workplace? What would it look like in your organization if every single employee was striving to be a part of the greater whole of the organization? Do you as a leader play a part in bringing this about? I say you do! You have a very large role in bringing this about. The way you communicate you're the vision and mission of the organization, the inspiring and uplifting words you use, the way you encourage the people at all levels of the organization, and the way you focus on positives rather than negatives can make a huge difference.

Part of the Scientific Management approach, intended or not, was a focus on the negative, a focus on the problems within the organization and working to correct those problems. What we need to do instead, is focus on the positives, the things that are really working well, and striving to build more of those positives in the organization. The former creates an atmosphere of negativity and depleted energy, whereas the latter creates an uplifting environment where everyone is invigorated and always looking for ways to improve the organization

"When nothing is sure,
everything is possible."
Margaret Drabble

rather than fix what is wrong. For years, we have had the wrong focus. David Cooperrider proved this in his doctoral thesis where he came up with the idea of Appreciative Inquiry which has had very dramatic effects around the World. Cooperrider, while working on research for his thesis was working at a health clinic in Cleveland, OH was originally focusing on problem solving. After a period of time, he met with his advisor and said he wanted to change his approach because he found that when an organization focuses on problem solving they always find a plethora of problems to work on. The more they looked for problems, the more problems they found. The other thing he noticed was that the more problems they found, the more the energy within the organization seemed to dissipate. Workers were becoming discouraged and disheartened. Cooperrider wanted to change his focus to a more positive approach by focusing on what was right in the organization. After getting approval to make the change in his thesis, he discovered that the more employees in the clinic talked about why they came to work for the clinic and what they liked about working there the energy level began to skyrocket. He began asking questions about peak moments employees had experienced and what was happening within the organization that allowed these peak moments to occur. He then brought everyone together to share their stories and from those stories, the organization determined its vision and goals/objectives to move the organization in alignment with allowing more peak moments to occur. As a result, employees regained their energy and enthusiasm for what they were doing and became more

"Blessed is the leader who seeks the best for those he serves."

Unknown

actively involved in their jobs and with their clients. Cooperrider's Appreciative Inquiry has since been recognized as a positive approach to organizational development by a wide variety of organizations from GTE, before its merger and name change to Verizon, and even the US Navy which has recently gone through an AI with Admirals and First lower level Seamen serving on jointly on teams to determine how to build a world class navy of the future. Organizations that have completed the AI process have reported dramatic gains in focus, employee engagement as well as an increase in profits.

Along with the evolution of society, business, and the world in general, the average American worker has greatly evolved as well. Today's average worker is vastly different from her counterpart 100 years ago. Today's workers want more from their job than just a paycheck. Now don't get me wrong, pay is important. Everyone needs to get a paycheck but that is not necessarily why people are working for today. I often asked the students in my classes, "How many work for money?" Of course many would raise their hands, if not all, and then I would ask, "How many work strictly for money?" and a majority of hands would go down. We would then follow up with a discussion on what they were looking for from their jobs: a sense of accomplishment, being a part of something greater than themselves, being able to use heart and mind, as well as many other statements reflecting higher order needs. In these discussions, did students reflect a growing sense of spirituality in the workplace? I believe so!

"Be the change you want to see in the world."
Mahatma Gandhi

Why Now?

Is the study of leadership more important today than in the past, and if so, why? The average worker of today is vastly different than ever before and he/she is demanding a different model of workplace interaction, workers today are wanting something different from their employment relationships and those entering the workforce seem intent on moving on to another organization if they do not find what they want. There seems to be a demand for better leadership. The average worker today wants to be led and not managed. Manage projects, budgets, departments, but do NOT try to manage people. Instead, lead them. Coach and mentor them. Support them and assist them in finding the better part of who they are and how they can contribute in a higher order. Today's workers are looking for leaders who focus on the positive, on what's right in the organization and in them and then striving to achieve more of what's right.

On May 28, 2008, CBS' 60 Minutes did a piece on the new generation in the workforce and how organizations are finding it difficult to deal with these new workers. According to Morley Safer, those entering the workforce today feel that they are special and expect to be treated as such. When they were young, they played on little league and other teams where there were no winners, no losers, and no score. Everyone received a trophy, plaque or certificate simply for being on the team. They were awarded for being special without knowing why they were special. They also grew up seeing their parents

"If I have seen farther than others, it is because I was standing on the shoulders of giants."

Sir Isaac Newton

staying at the same company for decades, working at jobs they didn't particularly like, and often working for bosses who mistreated and even abused them, and then get laid off late in their careers. Today's workers say they are not going to put up with that. They want careers that are meaningful for them today. In my generation, a meaningful career meant getting a long term job with a good company that paid well. For the majority of Baby Boomers, a career meant working for the same company throughout their working career, and it often meant doing work that was not particularly enjoyable, but liking what we did was not the focus of why we were there. We were there to make a living and support our families.

Milennials expect to be treated openly and honestly and recognized for what they can contribute to the organization. They have little patience for bureaucracy, nor are they willing to accept an autocratic or overly demanding supervisor/manager who gives little support, praise or appreciation.

If those entering the workforce today are unable to find what they are looking for in one company, they will quit and go somewhere else. They see nothing wrong with moving from job to job, often with 4-6 companies on their resume in one year and they see their main goal as finding the right place to offer their vast skills and talents. Today's workers also grew up in the digital age. Multi-tasking, computers and getting things done are all part of the skills they bring to the table and they are impatient and do not want to be put off, waiting for that

"You do not lead by hitting people over the head – that's assault, not leadership."
Dwight Eisenhower

day in the future, which may never come, when they can achieve a meaningful position. They expect more from their job, their supervisor and they want what they want. To many in the Baby Boomer generation, especially those in a supervisory or management position, this totally alien to anything they have experienced and they are struggling in learning how to deal with these young upstarts who are demanding they change and change now!

In many of the organizations in which I conduct a class on leadership, I typically hear, "My supervisor and manager need to be in this class!" "They need to be hearing what you are telling us about leadership and how things are changing, we believe it, we feel it, we see it, but we don't see it in our leaders!" To say that workers today are frustrated is a gross understatement. They hear about the need for better leadership, and the latest principles of leadership, and they relate how strongly they feel the same need, but sadly, those in supervisory or manager positions are not changing rapidly enough. As a Nation, we absolutely MUST change the way we do business. The larger the organization, the more this seems to be the case. Often, those at the very top understand the need for changes in leadership and they seem to have their finger on the pulse of the younger worker. They realize a need for a focus on training throughout the organization; however, it does not seem to be getting done in a progressive manner. By starting at the lowest level and teaching the principles of leadership seems to be doing little but creating frustration.

"Not everything that is faced can be changed. But nothing can be changed until it is faced."

James Baldwin

Although those in the training understand and agree with what is being taught, they have little opportunity to apply what they learn because of the decades of the "old ways" that have become part of everyday life. In order to really make a change in leadership, the system itself has to change. There must be deep change throughout every part of the organization. To do that, an organization must decide on exactly where it wants to go, (vision) and what is needed to get there and then the training, followed by accountability, begins at the top, the very top, and then goes down through every level, with changes in behavior, as a result of the training, being expected from each and every person. Performance evaluation systems need to be designed to reflect these needed behavior changes. Intensive training needs to be implemented in understanding personality theories, coaching, mentoring and communication. We have to start now at looking how we can engage our workers and bring more passion and enthusiasm to what they are doing. The impact if we don't, will be to lose more ground in world leadership. China and India are investing massive amounts of money on education and training and are reaping great benefits as a result.

We need a revolution in Leadership, and a revolution of the working environment, as well as a revolution of the systems that have been in place for decades. It is imperative to begin an all out, full-scale drive to educate, train and create leaders at all levels within an organization and at the same time, provide an environment in which theses leaders can thrive and grow.

"We must do all that we can, to give our children the best in education and social upbringing - for while they are the youth of today, they shall be the leaders of tomorrow."

John F. Kennedy

One of the greatest reasons these supervisors and managers are not getting the picture is how they were selected in the past. In many organizations I hear that promotions were granted primarily on the basis of seniority. Those who lasted the longest got the promotion. In the past there was very little, if any, thought given to the competencies needed in working with people, understanding people and leading people to be a supervisor or manager. The thought of the past seemed to be if someone was good at the current job and knew what they were doing then they would be a good supervisor. People skills, communication skills, and education level seemed to take a backseat in many organizations to longevity. Being able to think strategically and systemically were hardly thought of, especially at the supervisory level, after all, that certainly was not part of a supervisor's job in the past. Their job was to keep tabs on their workers and to see that they performed their jobs the way they were told. Today's workers are not willing to accept that way of thinking any longer. I hear a great level of frustration, disillusionment and even anger throughout many organizations. I hear that there is a very strong desire to see a change in leadership and today's workers want to be a part of that change.

Some organizations are slowly beginning to adapt to a new leadership style, but their efforts are, in some cases, too little too late! By the very fact that employees are expressing their frustration by saying their supervisor or manager should be hearing what they are hearing indicates that the organization is attempting to make

"Good leaders make people feel that they're at the very heart of things, not at the periphery. Everyone feels that he or she makes a difference to the success of the organization. When that happens people feel centered and that gives their work meaning."

Warren Bennis

changes but in American business, it seems that there is a feeling that as long as we do something to look like we are changing then that is enough. NO! It is not enough! Not by a long shot! Leadership starts at the top! Whatever is going on in an organization, good, bad or in between, lies squarely at the feet of the person at the top of the organization. It is time for the CEO's and other top people to come out of their ivory towers, learn that leadership today is not about them, but about the people they are leading and listen to the people throughout their organization to get a true understanding of what is going on.

An interesting show currently on television is "Undercover Boss" where the CEO goes undercover in his or her organization and works as an entry-level employee to gain an understanding of what is really going on. In show after show, CEO's are stating, "I had no idea what was happening!" In one recent episode, the CEO told his employees, "This experienced has changed me deeply from this point forward in my life." This is great, but in every case, actions speak louder than words. Leadership is about actions, as well as inspiring words!

One organization with whom I worked, conducted an all-employee survey and one of the questions was, "Can you do more on your job?" An amazingly large percentage of employees responded, "Yes" In talking to people throughout the organization I came to understand this to be a recognition that they had a desire to be more a part of what they were doing and could offer more in how the work was done. Again, in my conversations with many

"The leader has to be practical and a realist, yet must talk the language of the visionary and the idealist."

Eric Hoffer

employees throughout the company the more they felt they could do, was to be more involved, to offer more insight as to how the job could be done, how they could be more efficient and productive. However, unfortunately, the COO believed this to mean that people within the organization did not have enough work to keep them busy and so he put a freeze on filling positions. Some months after I was no longer associated with this company I ran into a manager with whom I had previously worked and he informed me that people were leaving the company in large numbers because supervisors and managers were being required to work ten and twelve hour days because positions were not being filled.

STAR leaders work to build their employees, at all levels, and coach them to better performance by helping them see areas THEY want to work on for improvement. STAR leaders see the best in their employees and strive to help those employees see the best in themselves. The COO, unfortunately, expressed his belief on different occasions about the employees taking advantage and not wanting to work and fell way short of being a STAR Leader.

STAR Leadership is about being in tune with your organization and with your followers. It is about focusing your energy on where you want to go and what you want your organization to become and believing in the power and potential of everyone throughout your organization to make it happen. It is about creating a vision and letting your followers figure out how to make it happen. It is about knowing as much as you can about

"People of the world don't look at themselves, and so they blame one another."

Mevlana Rumi

yourself and why you do what you do, so you can better understand those who choose to follow you. STAR Leadership is about having the ability to communicate a clear focus on where you want to go and about listening to others. It is also about interacting with others with caring, having empathy and it is about coaching others to better performance, rather than driving others to simply do more. It is also being willing to be coached from others throughout your organization. Being a STAR Leader is about opening your heart, your creative brain, and seeing with a greater vision. STAR Leaders know that it is also about how you perceive yourself and learning how others perceive you. STAR Leadership is also about recognizing emotions and their impact on how you interact with others and how others interact in the workplace.

The Evolution of the Average Worker

Many of today's management systems are based on theories that are decades old, some having changed little since their inception. In many of my classes, I lead participants through an exercise of understanding in which we discuss the criteria with which we might use to determine the "average" employee. Some of the criteria on which we focused were age, gender, education, ethnicity, experience/skills and general world-view. I then divide the class into two sections of table groups and ask them to discuss in their groups these criteria and to arrive at a general profile of the "average" worker. The only difference is that half of the groups are asked to

"People ask the difference between a leader and a boss. The leader works in the open and the boss in covert. The leader leads and the boss drives."

Theodore Roosevelt

do this for the "average" worker of today, and the other half were asked to do the same thing for the average worker 100 years ago.

Fig. 2 shows an approximation of what most groups came up with. Although there may be some argument in some areas, I think these approximations come fairly close. I have been unable to find any data that was collected in 1909 but it is certainly not difficult to imagine what some of these criteria might have been when we look at each of them independently. In 1909, there were no child labor laws in the U.S., the average life expectancy in 1904 is said to have been 47 years, so it is reasonably safe to assume that the age of the average worker would be significantly lower than today's workforce where children are not allowed to work in many situations, and the average life expectancy is in the low eighties with many people of the baby boomer generation working well beyond what was considered just a few short years ago as the 'normal' retirement age.

Certainly, the education level in 1909 was significantly lower than it is today. We could be doing much better in the education arena today, especially in the inner cities of this country where the drop-out rate is hovering just above 50%, according to many studies. For African American males, that figures rises in some areas to around 70% which I find to be absolutely atrocious. However, it is not unheard of for many, if not the majority of workers today to have some education beyond high-school. It may be some college or a trade school, but on average we are a much better educated

"I start with the premise that the function of leadership is to produce more leaders, not more followers."

Ralph Nader

society than in the past. One hundred years ago, education was considered a luxury for those with money. For the average person, education took away from the focus of making money and putting food on the table. My father was born in 1908 and he only attended school through the 6th grade. I was told that he did not go further because his father thought that education, beyond being able to read and write, was a waste of time.

Criteria	1909	2009
Age	20's – 30's	40's – 50's
Education	6th grade or less	High School +
Gender	95% M/5% F	50%M/50%F
Ethnicity	90% + White	60% W/40% NW
Experience	Little to none	Highly Skilled
World View	20 mile radius	The World

Fig. 2

Another simple fact of life, 100 years ago, was that a woman typically did not work outside the home, unless she was unmarried and had no other means of support, and then the jobs open to women were typically menial, domestic, or "women" oriented jobs such as cooking, cleaning, or taking care of children. It was not until World War II that women began doing jobs typically considered the domain of men. With the majority of men in the U.S. in Europe fighting the war, women began

"Leadership is not so much about technique and methods, as it is about opening the heart. Leadership is about inspiration -- of oneself and of others. Great leadership is about human experiences, not processes. Leadership is not a formula or a program, it is a human activity that comes from the heart and considers the hearts of others. It is an attitude, not a routine."

Lance Secretan

filling the factories across the country and "Rosie the Riveter" came into being and became a driving force in America's war effort. Although they were quickly replaced by the men returning home after the end of the war, women began to see that there were far more options for them than staying at home and they became increasingly less content to do so.

The ethnicity of the average worker one hundred years ago was most definitely predominately white. With segregation a part of a major portion of this country, people of color were denied the opportunity to get a decent job and earn a livable wage. . Of course, this was not an absolute but a general trend. It wasn't until many decades later that laws were enacted to correct great wrongs in employment practices as well as societal practices. Today, cultural diversity is a mainstay of most organizations. I'm not saying that prejudice and discrimination are a thing of the past, for they are not, however great strides have been made and leaders today must continue to focus attention on creating an open and fair hiring/working environment for all people. The skills, abilities, education and talents that someone brings to the job is all that should matter, not the color of their skin, their religion, sexual orientation or any other non-work related issue.

A century ago, workers were leaving the farms in large numbers and going to cities all across America in search of a better way of life. Being that they were young with little or no education, they did not bring a great deal of experience that could be used on their job. Having

"Outstanding leaders go out of the way to boost the self-esteem of their personnel. If people believe in themselves, it's amazing what they can accomplish."

Sam Walton

grown up in an agrarian environment, many of their skills did not easily translate to the factory floor. In today's work environment there is a greater focus on technology, regardless of the industry and today's workers bring a great deal of technological experience, knowledge and education, as well as a greater understanding of the world around them.

This knowledge of the world, and what it imparts to the average worker and how it impacts his/her view of his/her place in society is something I find of great interest. One hundred years ago, the world view of the average worker was what was taking place within, most likely, a 20 mile radius of where he worked and lived. I truly doubt that many workers 100 years ago knew or even cared much about places like Iraq, Afghanistan, or other exotic places. Their world truly was where they lived and worked. Today's average worker not only is aware of these places, but many workers have been to these place and many others outside of the U.S. We are truly living in a global village, where instant communication with anyone, anywhere in the world is at our fingertips. This, I believe, brings with it a much deeper understanding of the world in general and creates a more cognizant and mature worker.

In the exercise I have do in my classes where we look at the average worker then vs. now, I focus on 100 years ago for a very specific reason. Something rather specific and very significant happened a little over 100 years ago. In 1908, Henry Ford opened the first mass production,

"As we, the leaders, deal with tomorrow, our task is not to try to make perfect plans. …Our task is to create organizations that are sufficiently flexible and versatile that they can take our imperfect plans and make them work in execution. That is the essential character of the learning organization."

Gordon R. Sullivan & Michael V. Harper

assembly-line, automobile manufacturing plant. In doing so, Ford did a couple of things differently. First, at the horror of fellow business leaders, Ford paid his workers a almost twice the prevailing wage of the day. Why did he do this? For the simple reason that he wanted his workers to make enough money to be able to buy the product they were producing, thereby getting more automobiles on the street! Secondly, Ford hired an industrial engineer, by the name of Frederick Taylor. Taylor was a time and motion study specialist and his role was to devise a management system in which the plant could operate the most efficiently. Taylor's work came to be known as Scientific Management or in later years as Theory X. Taylor recognized that in order to keep workers focused on their job, supervisors needed to be watching over them, seeing that they were doing their jobs properly and be ready to lend assistance if needed. Taylor devised a span-of-control system in which a supervisor could only adequately supervise a limited number of workers, assistant managers could only supervise a limited number of supervisors and managers could only supervise so many assistant managers. Jobs were devised so that the uneducated worker would perform a simple repetitive tasks without having to think about what they were doing. Down the line, everyone at each level was expected to do exactly as they were told with no deviation. I would imagine that it was not a part of the workers' psyche to even question what they were being told to do. Since Ford paid his workers almost double the pay of the average of the day, the desire to work for Ford was much greater. This provided Ford with the luxury of quickly replacing any worker that did

"The only real training for leadership is leadership."

Anthony Jay

not want to do what he was told, thereby keeping production high.

Motivation Theories

I have always been fascinated by people. Fascinated at what makes people do what they do. I remember studying about Frederick Taylor in college and his Scientific Management theory and then reading about the studies at the Western Electric Hawthorn plant. Those conducting the studies were interested in learning what they could do to the environment to speed up production. The Hawthorne plant was a piece-work plant were workers were paid by the number of pieces they assembled. Up to this time, there was very little, if any, thought given to the worker themselves and what they might be contributing to the production process other than their ability to assemble the parts. It was all about the process and the environment that contributed to productivity, and not the workers, so this is where those conducting the tests were focused. After separating a test group form a control group, one study began by increasing the lighting in the plant. Those conducting the test were pleasantly surprised that productivity went up. Increasing the lighting seemed like a rather simple thing to do to get increased productivity! So, in order to test their theory that increased lighting was indeed the factor to increase productivity, they decreased the lighting and were very surprised to learn that productivity went up again, instead of going down as they had expected.

Out of the Hawthorne Studies, came an enlightening understanding of the role the worker himself played in

"Never hire or promote in your own image. It is foolish to replicate your strength and idiotic to replicate your weakness. It is essential to employ, trust, and reward those whose perspective, ability and judgment are radically different from yours. It is also rare, for it requires uncommon humility, tolerance, and wisdom."

Dee Hock

the increase of productivity. This led to a whole new generation of studies directed at the workers themselves. In the 1950's and 1960's it was Douglas MacGregor, Frederick Herzberg, David McClelland, B.F. Skinner and others who studied different aspects of human motivation, each offering their own take on what motivated people in the work environment, all focused on improving productivity, as before, but this time, the focus was on the individual employee. The greatest of these theorists, or at least the one that has always greatly influenced my thinking, was Abraham Maslow and his Hierarchy of Needs theory (see Fig. 3). Although I always felt a connection to Maslow and seemed to understand at a deeper level that he was correct in his theory, it wasn't until I began really focusing on the differences between the average worker of today and his counterpart of 100 years ago that it all came together for me.

Although there may be much argument about my loose interpretations, I believe that we can look at the evolution of the average worker through Maslow's hierarchy and see some striking comparisons. In the early days of the 20th century, the primary reason people worked was for one simple reason – to put food on the table and provide shelter for their families, i.e. Maslow's lowest level, physiological needs. Although there were other reasons, for a majority of workers it was simply to earn a living and they didn't think about much else. As we move forward, into the 1930's, following the National Recovery Act, in 1933 workers began to organize on a

*"And when we think we lead,
we are most led."*

Lord Byron

greater scale and one of unions' primary focuses at the time was worker safety. As workers began to feel more

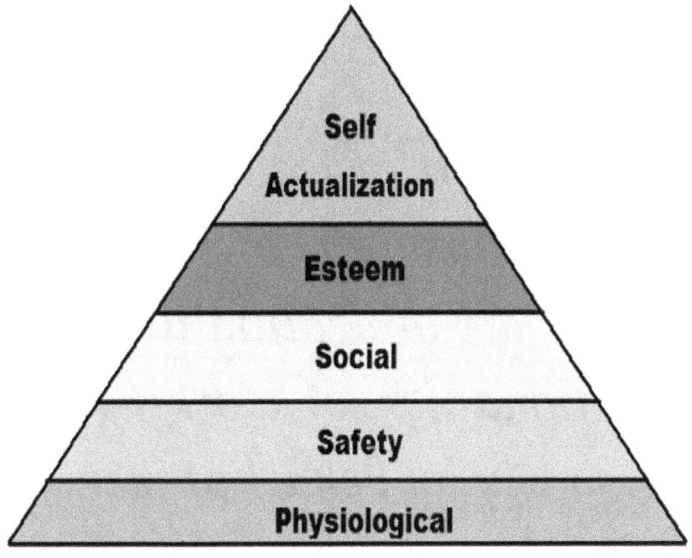

Fig. 2

secure in their income, (Ford's willingness to pay his workers a wage almost double that of the prevailing rate helped in this area) and in their ability to provide for the basic needs of their family, they began to focus on their own personal safety on the job as well as the safety of their income, hence their interest in and involvement in unions and obtaining a safe work environment.

As unions continued to grow, and workers' physiological needs and safety issues were being met, things took a dramatic turn after WW-II. As men returned from the war and returned to their jobs, this country experienced a

"The art of leading, in operations large or small, is the art of dealing with humanity, of working diligently on behalf of men, of being sympathetic with them, but equally, of insisting that they make a square facing toward their own problems."

S.L.A. Marshall

great boom period, new houses were being built at an incredible rate, the economy was growing and there was an increased focus on becoming more social. Many organizations began to form employee clubs, sports teams and provide other opportunities in which employees could socialize and get to know each other outside of work. Things were good and employees were enjoying a totally different lifestyle than their predecessors and they focused their attention on socializing with their fellow employees. Maslow's theory says that this is our need for belonging, of being a part of something and building friendships. I remember the company I began working for in 1967 had many different employee clubs which encouraged members to socialize in different contexts. The company even had a physical employee club with a dining hall, where employees could have dinner in the evening and get acquainted with the each other's spouse and children. It softball diamonds, tennis courts, bar-be-cue grills, and an outdoor theater, where movies were shown every Friday night for free, all in an attempt to meet the social needs (Maslow's level 3) of the employees. I find it interesting to note that the focus on these types of social clubs within organizations is difficult to find anymore. Many organizations, including the one I first worked for, have now abolished these types of clubs. Also, it is interesting that the late 1980's and the 1990's were known as the "Me" generation where the focus was on the individual and what he or she could acquire. The private parking space, the corner office, the special job title, bonuses or other perks can possibly be seen as focusing on esteem needs. During this time, the focus was on "Look at me!"

"Jingshen is the Mandarin word for spirit and vivacity. It is an important word for those who would lead, because above all things, spirit and vivacity set effective organizations apart from those that will decline and die."

James L. Hayes

"See me!" or "Notice who I am!" Certainly seems to imply that Maslow's level 4, esteem needs, was very much in action during this time. Recently, I discussed Maslow and his hierarchy and the evolution of the average American worker in a leadership development class I was facilitating and found a great deal of interest in the topic. The following morning, I asked if anyone had thought about the topics we discussed the previous day and what thoughts they had on our discussion. One woman said that on her way home she began to think about Maslow's hierarchy and where she saw herself in the pyramid. She said, "I have been planning on buying a new car and I have been planning on buying the nicest Lexus I could find, top of the line, and I realized, after our discussion yesterday, that I wanted that car in order for other people to notice me and as a way to boost my self-esteem." She went on to say something I considered to be quite profound, "The more I thought about it, I realized that I did not need a car to boost my self-esteem. I did not need a car to be noticed and I have decided that I am going to start looking at a much different car and begin to focus on other aspects of my life." I found this to be profound because it indicated a great step in personal growth and awareness. As you will see later, this growth in personal understanding and awareness is a foundation of being a STAR Leader of the future.

Today, we live in a totally different world than the workers of 100 years ago. In each new generation since that time children have grown up with a totally different environment than the one in which their parents grew up. Each generation began at a level much higher in under-

"The quality of a leader is reflected in the standards they set for themselves."

Ray Kroc

standing and comprehension that generations before. So the question I ask, "Is the average worker today focused on Maslow's Level 5, Self-Accualization, or at least approaching this level?" Today's workers have repeatedly said they want to be a part of something greater than themselves. When I taught Organizational Behavior in the MBA program the same text was used for many years, with periodic updates resulting in a revised edition. In the last text I used in this class, there was a section unlike any section I had seen in that book, or in any other text for that matter. It was a section on Spirituality in the Workplace! The authors stated that the focus on spirituality did not mean a focus on religion, but a focus on being a part of something greater. They noted that there is a growing sense on the part of workers of a need to be part of something greater than themselves. This sounds very much like Maslow's highest order need! Today's workers want to bring the totality of who they are to the job. They no longer want to be told what to do, when to do it, and how to do it like the workers 100 years ago experienced. Today's workers are much better educated, bring far more to the job than in the past and want to jump into their job with both feet and work as much with their heads and their hearts as they do with their hands. I have had the opportunity to interact with a wide variety of workers both in the office and the manufacturing plant floor, public and private organizations and I consistently hear the same thing: A need to be a part of and engaged in what is going on around them.

"If I can conceive it,
I can see it.
If I can see it,
I can believe it.
If I can believe it,
I can create it."
Unknown

So, if the average worker is approaching the top of Maslow's hierarchy, what does this mean, to them and to the role of the leader? It means that the days of telling someone what to do and how to do it are gone. The time of the micro-manager is over! No longer will workers be willing to "follow" a leader who is going nowhere or at least doesn't say where they are going and why. Workers today are looking for STAR Leaders who have a clear vision of where they want to go and who have the ability to communicate that vision in ways that inspire, support, and encourage. Followers are looking for STAR Leaders who have the ability to coach them to better performance, STAR Leaders who consider the workers' welfare to be a top priority. Gone are the days of the autocratic style that tells rather than asks, that demands rather than supports, and that thinks that workers must be "managed" in order to achieve success. The success of organizations today lies in the hearts and minds of everyone who is a part of the organization, and not just those at the top of the organization. There is such tremendous potential going untapped in organizations everywhere because of the inability or unwillingness to change to a different style of management. The fear of changing is leading to the demise of far too many organizations and in today's world, we must do everything we can if we are going to continue to compete in the global marketplace.

Core Competencies of Leadership

In order to learn about leadership, we need to first understand exactly what the elements are that we need to

"'Cheshire Puss'.......would you tell me please, which way I ought to go from here?' 'That depends a good deal on where you want to get to,' said the Cat. 'I don't much care where—' said Alice. 'Then it doesn't matter which way you go,' said the Cat. '—so long as I get somewhere,' Alice added as an explanation. 'Oh, you're sure to do that,' said the cat, 'if you only walk long enough.'"

Lewis G. Carroll
"Through the Looking Glass"

learn. Every job has core competencies, those basic elements that someone must possess in order to do that particular job in a competent manner. For some jobs, such as an airline pilot, those basic elements are easy to determine. The pilot must be able to fly an aircraft safely, including taxiing, taking off and landing without damaging the airplane or injuring his passengers. For a school teacher, he or she must be able to understand the basic concepts of learning, communicate effectively, manage a classroom, and teach a particular subject in a way that the students can comprehend what is being taught. In both cases, there are particular skills that can be learned. One's proficiency at either job would depend on his or her individual skills, adaptability, as well as his or her willingness to continue to learn and improve.

However, there are those occupations such as Leader, where the core competencies may be a little more difficult to determine. Much has been written about leadership and about what other writers feel are the most important aspects of leadership; so again, unlike the role of an airline pilot or a school teacher the core competencies for leadership are mainly open for discussion and disagreement. The core competencies I am presenting here are not a result of great in-depth study, or based on scientific research, but are based on my understanding of Leadership, and my reading different literature and the many discussions I have had in my classes as well as outside of the University and of course, on my experiences working with a wide variety of leaders. The eight core competencies of Leadership that I believe to be the most important are represented in

"The most pathetic person in the world is the one who has sight but no vision."
Helen Keller

what I call *"The STAR Leadership Star"* (Fig. 1). I will briefly discus each of the eight competencies here and will cover each one in more depth in the ensuing chapters.

Vision – Vision gives everyone in the organization a roadmap of where the leader is going and a clear reason for going there. It is the *numero uno,* the most important, the "without it you're not a leader" of core competencies. I believe that it is absolutely impossible for someone to be considered a leader if they do not have a clear vision of what they want to accomplish. Without a clear sense of where he or she wants to go, the organization, and/or his followers will meander around, and will likely end up somewhere other than where the leader feels they should be. Without a vision, you or your organization will definitely end up somewhere, but is it where you want it to be?

Integrity – Although moral integrity is becoming increasingly more important in today's business world, especially with the recent problems on Wall St. and the ensuing economic collapse, in this sense, integrity means, in the words of W. Edwards Deming, "constancy of purpose". Far too often, an organizational leader will state his/her vision for where they want their organization to go and expect the organization to immediately fall in line and do what is needed to accomplish that vision. In reality, however, what often happens is the organization is not properly aligned, reward systems run counter to what is needed, and employees in different areas of the company understand the vision differently and often work in opposite

"To effectively communicate, we must realize that we are all different in the way we perceive the world and use this understanding as a guide to our communication with others."

Tony Robbins

STAR Leadership Star

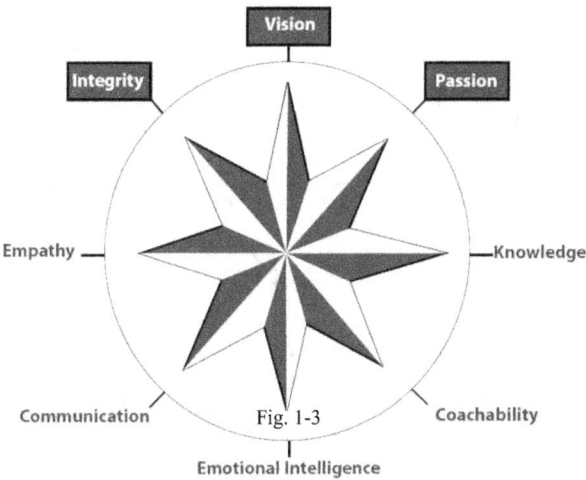

Fig. 1-3

directions, causing the Leader to wonder what went wrong. Integrity tells everyone that whatever they do, it must be aligned with the vision and the entire organization must work as one unit, together, as a team to accomplish the vision. Integrity means that nothing is done in the organization unless it is in an effort to accomplish the vision

Passion – If the leader of the organization isn't passionate about accomplishing the vision, why in the world would anyone else be interested? After all, it is the leader's vision, isn't it? There is an overwhelming power, mostly untapped, that exists in every organization. The power of the people who work there!

"I am personally convinced that one person can be a change catalyst, a "transformer" in any situation, any organization. Such an individual is yeast that can leaven an entire loaf. It requires vision, initiative, patience, respect, persistence, courage, and faith to be a transforming leader."

Stephen Covey

There is something truly magical when passion is ignited and people become involved because they want to rather than because they are being paid to. We become energized and relate to the world around us on an entirely different level. Deeply caring about where you want to go and what you want to achieve is crucial. Being open about that passion and displaying that it at every opportunity is vital to success. Your passion instills in others the awareness that this is something important and something that needs to be accomplished. It help create the feeling in others that this is a place they want to go. Passion speaks volumes about how important the vision is. Passion is the fuel for the fire! Without passion, life is a very dull existence. With passion, we become alive!

Empathy – Having a deep understanding and caring about the people who make up the organization is, I believe, key to bringing everyone together with a cohesive focus. In order for a leader to lead, they need to know and understand themselves and other people. Above all, it is critical that he or she knows and understands himself/herself. They must know who they are and why they do the things they do, for that will give them a better understanding of their followers. Genuinely caring for and showing empathy for others in your organization allows others to see that you care about them and their well-being.

Knowledge – Leaders today must be on a quest for knowledge. They need knowledge, not only about themselves, but about the market trends, and people within the organization. They need knowledge about

"A great leader's courage to fulfill his vision comes from passion, not position."
John Maxwell

their own area of expertise and how to apply that knowledge. They must constantly be seeking to learn about how they themselves can be better at what they do. I am sure that if I asked any organization's CEO, whether or not they want their employee's to constantly improve at their jobs, they would all answer with a resounding YES!

Yet, how many of those CEO's do you believe are continuously focused on their own improvement? In a vast number of organizations, those at the top are so busy working IN the business, they take little time to work ON the business. Leaders need to be continually learning about themselves and how they show up in the world, why they do the things they do, the style and manner in which they communicate with others and the impact of their style of communicating. This is a huge area because the leader must continually increasing his/her knowledge about a great many things.

Communication – Undoubtedly, the ability to communicate is essential. It is key in everything we do and far too often, organizations lose valuable resources due to miscommunication, or lack of communication entirely.. It is one thing to have a great, inspiring vision, but if the leader is unable to communicate that vision, then it goes unfulfilled. It is estimated that $300,00.000,000 is lost annually in business due to miscommunication. That's approximately $1 Billion dollars each day!

"Absolute identity with one's cause is the first and great condition of successful leadership."

Woodrow Wilson

Emotional Intelligence -- Emotional intelligence has come to be recognized by many as a key factor in leadership. How an individual handles his or her emotions, how they understand the emotions of others and how they use their emotions effectively is essential in working in today's organizations.

Coach-ability -- This is not only the ability to coach others but to have the ability to be coached. Today's employees do NOT need to be managed, they are capable of managing themselves. They need to be coached to better performance and they want to be led! They need to be led by leaders who are capable of helping them see and then achieve greater potential within themselves.

At the same time, leaders need to be open to being coached by others: Those to whom they report, their peers, AND those who report to them. Performance can be greatly enhanced at all levels if an open, safe and supportive environment is created where there is a clear focus on working on building strengths of everyone and improving on those strengths.

Each of these core competencies will be explored in greater depth in following chapters, and although there may be many other key factors in leadership and other things that an effective leader must know and be able to do, I believe that these are the most important, with Vision, Integrity and Passion being the 3 most important.

"Always shoot for the moon, for even if you miss, you will be among the stars!"

Unknown

CHAPTER TWO

VISION

*[a: the act or power of imagination **b** (1): mode of seeing or conceiving (2): unusual discernment or foresight <a person of vision> c: direct mystical awareness of the supernatural usually in visible form]*

A Leader without vision is simply a manager!

What characteristics or attributes do these leaders share? George Washington, Nelson Mandela, George Patton, Mother Teresa, Adolph Hitler, John F. Kennedy, Genghis Kahn, Rev. Dr. Martin Luther King, Jr.? Drive, passion, vision, belief in what they were doing, ability to communicate and unrelenting drive to accomplish what they saw as possible. It is difficult to prioritize all of these important areas but clearly each had a very certain and distinct focus on where they wanted their organization/country to go, or something very specific they wanted to accomplish. They had a clear vision, a focused intention on what they wanted to see. It is difficult to imagine that the conditions under which Mother Teresa worked. Working in the slums of Calcutta, India with the untouchables of the Hindu caste system, lifting the sick and dying out of the sewage infested gutters, she cared for them with love and compassion, working tirelessly to show them dignity. How

"A vision is not just a picture of what could be; it is an appeal to our better selves, a call to become something more."

Rosabeth Moss Kanter

could she have possibly gotten others to work with her under those conditions unless she had great passion for a compelling vision, communicated that vision and allowed others to buy-in and participate in bringing that vision about?

Knowing where you are going, and having a clear, distinct vision of what that may look like is essential to leadership. Much as the Cheshire Cat said to Alice, if you don't know where you want to go, then it does not matter what road you take to get there. It does not matter what you do, and it does not matter what anyone else in your organization does. If a clear vision is not constantly kept in focus, communicated on a regular basis, and with a deep sense of urgency, with passion, to get there it is very unlikely that your vision will become a reality. Sadly, many "leaders" of the past believed that because they were the leader all they had to say was, in the words of Captain Jean Luc Picard of the starship enterprise on Star Trek The Next Generation, "make it so" and the organization would suddenly stop, re-focus, and align itself with what was ordered. Unfortunately, it did not happen then and it does not happen today.

If you keep working long enough and hard enough, you WILL end up somewhere. But the question is, is it where you really want your organization to be? Many times, I have heard leaders in organizations complain because they were unable to meet production demands, or employees weren't cooperating or "behaving" properly, or this isn't right, or that isn't working. When we focus on what is wrong in the organization we lose sight of our

"We are not limited by our abilities, but by our vision."
Unknown

vision, or our intention, and we are surprised when we do not achieve our vision. Not only do we not achieve our vision, but we seem to get more of the opposite of what we want to have happen. There is a rapidly growing recognition of the importance of focusing on what we want to have in our lives or in our organizations and not focusing on the things we don't want. From Appreciative Inquiry, finding out what employees got really excited about their jobs and building more of that in the company's goals and objectives by, David Cooperrider, Phd., to Asset Based Thinking, building on the strengths of the organization and the individual members by Kathryn Cramer of the Cramer Institute and StrengthsFinder 2.0 which focuses on identifying each individuals strengths and showing how matching those strengths to the task at hand, organizations around the world are making tremendous strides to build a positive, forward-thinking organization.

How do you know when you get there if you didn't know where you were going?

The ability to clearly see where you want to go and what it is going to take to get there is not always easy. Staying one hundred percent focused on where you want to go and what you WANT, takes continuous effort. Being able to clearly see where you want to go may sound easy, but it is often quite difficult. Knowing what it will take to get there is the least of the problem. Why? Because you have an organization full of creative, energetic, wise, courageous and inspired workers who want to go to the place you envision and can communicate clearly to them.

"Keep your dreams alive. Understand to achieve anything requires faith and belief in yourself, vision, hard work, determination, and dedication. Remember all things are possible for those who believe."

Gail Devers

Get everyone involved, let them use their creativity, inspire their passion and they will figure out exactly what it will take to reach your vision. Yes, that means that you do not have to constantly be in charge! Do not attempt to micro-manage the process or it will not work! I doubt rather seriously if any of the previously mentioned leaders had an idea of the challenges ahead and what they were specifically going to have to do in order to achieve their vision. When people really buy into a vision and become inspired by the leader, they are more than willing to find a way to make it happen. The power of creativity of the human mind is awe inspiring.

Your vision is the fuel that drives the engine that turns the wheels to drive where you want your organization to go. The passion you have for accomplishing your vision, and your ability to share that vision and generate passion in others is the spark that ignites the fuel. The world today would be in a very sad state of affairs if those before us had not had vision and a passionate drive to achieve new heights. Vision may be something as grand as solving world hunger, or as simple as acquiring a new degree or learning a new technique in your favorite hobby. Of course, the grander your vision, the greater the opportunity of inspiring others to be a part of your vision.

One of the greatest proclaimed visions of modern time was when President John F. Kennedy proclaimed on May 26, 1961, to a joint session of Congress, "By the end of this decade, we will put a man on the moon and return

"Do not follow where the path may lead. Go instead where there is no path and leave a trail."

Muriel Strode

him to earth safely." Andrea Nelson, Leadership Development Manager for a large aerospace defense contractor said, "A vision that is easily translated, presents a burning platform that compels action." President Kennedy's vision created that burning platform for the American public. America was in a race with the Soviets for space exploration and the Soviets had been the first to put a capsule into orbit around the earth, and on April 12, 1961 Yuri Alekseyevich Gagarin, a Soviet cosmonaut, became the first man to journey into outer space. Needless to say, there was a burning desire to be first at something and going to the moon was just the thing that inspired the imagination of a nation.

At the time, few people could even conceive the possibility of a man walking on the moon, let alone even reaching the moon. I'm certain that many of the aeronautical engineers that would be working on the project had their doubts that an endeavor such as going to the moon was even remotely possible. But on July 20, 1969, Neil Armstrong, stepped out of the lunar lander and became the first human to set foot on the moon, with the immortal words, "One small step for man, one giant leap for mankind."

WOW! What an accomplishment, never before in the history of the earth had something so grand ever been accomplished. Today, travel to space is becoming somewhat, routine, but in 1961, it truly was the new frontier and few could even conceive the possibility of things to come. Just a few simple words, spoken by a man in a leadership position inspired the imagination of a

"To the person who does not know where he wants to go, there is no favorable wind."
Seneca

generation, ignited their passion and the undisputed greatest achievement of the 20th century became a reality.

What was it about those few words that so inspired a nation to commit to doing the impossible? Was it simply because they were spoken by a President? I doubt that President Kennedy had any idea of how to accomplish a feat so extraordinary, however he was willing to believe in the creativity of the human mind. He was willing to trust in those whose job it was to figure out the details. He recognized that his job was to inspire, encourage, support, remove obstacles and provide the resources necessary to do the impossible. What is it about vision that we find so mesmerizing, so compelling, and at the same time so frightening? What is it that stirs in the depth of our being, the very heart of who we are, that incites us to dare to believe that the impossible may actually be accomplished? Since the beginning of time, the world has been on an evolutionary path. Early humans were far different than we are today. They did not have the capacity to think, understand, or do many of the things that today we take for granted, yet there was something innate that was constantly driving our species forward. Was there a part of early man's makeup that allowed, or even encouraged him to dream? Do we have a "vision" gene that is part of our DNA that enables us to envision new horizons, new vistas, and new opportunities? Dreaming, the art of seeing that which is not tangible, is what has forever driven us to greater heights, greater accomplishments. The ability to dream, to ask "what if?" must be part of being Human. A major role of leaders is to tap into that inherent, innate quality

"Destiny is not a matter of chance, but of choice. Not something to wish for, but to attain."

William Jennings Bryan

of their followers, help them see what is possible to accomplish and allow them to be a part of something greater than themselves.

What are the things you dream of accomplishing? Everyone has dreams, what are yours? Do you routinely challenge yourself to dream big? When was the last time you took the time to sit and just dream of where you or your organization could go, of what you could accomplish, of what it would feel like if you accomplished something truly amazing? Remember, a vision can be something on a grand, world-wide scale, or something as simple as going on that special vacation. It could be as big as seeing your company become THE number one company in your segment of the business world, or it could be as simple as a goal for the number of Girl Scout cookies your troop sells. What are your intentions? What is it you truly believe is possible to achieve? What would you like to accomplish, but maybe do not believe is achievable? Maybe, just maybe, if you dare to dream big, and believe that everything is possible, those who choose to follow may surprise you in what they can accomplish.

The Power of Vision

I grew up in a very small town of 300 people in Southeast Missouri. When I was five years old, my parents, two older brothers and I moved to Berkeley, California, where my father's sister and her family lived. My father was able to get a very good job and we lived fairly well. I started Kindergarten shortly after we

"*Dream lofty dreams, and as you dream, so shall you become. Your Vision is the promise of what you shall one day be. Your Ideal is the prophecy of what you shall at last unveil.*"

Allen James

arrived and when I was 9 years old, my parents decided to move back to the area where I was born and my life changed dramatically. The school system in Berkeley was quite large and I remember that the grade school I attended ran split shifts to accommodate all of the students. When we moved back to MO, we first lived in Hunter, MO, with a population of 105. We lived in a house with neither electricity nor running water and I attended school in a two-room schoolhouse with grades 1-4 in one room and grades 5-8 in the other. The school also did not have an indoor bathroom. I thought my world had ended! Although my father had a very good job in California, both of my parents desperately missed the area where they were born and raised. In fact, I later found out that my father's ancestors first settled in that area in 1830, so the area had almost become part of our family's DNA. Other than the amenities of life, jobs were also very hard to come by. My father had only a sixth-grade education and did not have many marketable skills other than the ability to work hard. So, at the age of nine I learned very quickly the meaning of hard work. Opportunities to earn a living were very limited so my father began doing whatever he could to earn money. One of the first things he did was cut and sell firewood, the main method of heating homes in the area at the time. He would cut and split the wood while my brother and I would load it onto the truck and then carry and stack it for those who bought the wood from us.

There was a company in town which had several large kilns where they produced charcoal. Charcoal was pro-

"Big thinking precedes great achievement."
Wilferd Peterson

duced by loading a very large concrete kiln with freshly cut wood, igniting a fire, closing the doors to the kiln and letting the fire smolder in a controlled environment for several days. The wood purchased for this endeavor was bought from whoever was hardy enough to cut and haul the wood to the kilns. I soon discovered that we were hardy enough to do just that although I would have rather do something else!. At this same time, I took on the job of delivering the daily newspaper, produced in a short distance away, to over 50 homes in town. My days, during summer vacations from school involved getting up very early and going to the woods where we would cut and load about 3 cord of wood to be delivered to the charcoal kilns, followed by various odd jobs, which would then be followed by my paper route, which I would either walk or ride my bike. HARD WORK to be sure, and I grew up with a vision of doing something different with my life! I wasn't sure what, but I soon understood that if I was going to have a life better than the one my father had, I had to get an education! My vision became that I would somehow go to college and get a degree, although we had no money and I had no idea how to get the money I needed to achieve my vision! I wasn't sure which field of study I wanted to enter, however I was certain I wanted to get an education and to be able to live better than we were living at the time. Whatever I did, it would NOT involve cutting wood! I maintained my vision, and although my ability to get a degree did not come about for several years, I did manage to not only achieve an undergraduate degree but a Masters as well. Today, a Master's degree is comparable to an undergraduate degree was when I

"Cherish your visions and your dreams, as they are the children of your soul, the blueprints of your ultimate achievements."

Napoleon Hill

achieved my Master's as there is an ever increasing focus on achieving a higher education, which means the work-force is continually increasing in knowledge and education.

About this same time I experienced another opportunity to appreciate the importance of having a vision. During the summer between my junior and senior years of high school, I was visiting my sister and her family in St. Louis. 1966 was the year of some of the coolest cars to ever drive the streets! The car I dreamed of owning was a Mustang. I can still remember the feeling I would get when I would see a Mustang driving by, the feeling that someday I would have one of my own. During that visit, I was riding in the car with my sister when we passed an apartment complex that I always thought would be a great place to live. It was new, air conditioned (one of my main goals) and it had a swimming pool! What more could a poor boy from the country hope for? As we were passing the apartments, a Mustang pulled up beside us and I began to "see" me living in one of those apartments, driving a Mustang, and making at least $10,000 per year, a good wage at that time for someone my age. The vision became almost over-powering. The feeling was so strong, I can still remember it today so many years later. As it turned out, within two years, without even giving it much thought, I found myself living in one of those apartments, driving a Mustang and earning more than the $10,000 per year I had imagined. Although this was a personal vision that did not involve inspiring others, a leaders vision, if it is clear, inspiring and communicated on a constant and regular basis can

"Dissatisfaction and discouragement are not caused by the absence of things but the absence of vision."

Anonymous

and will be fulfilled by those willing to follow. The power of dreams, visions, is compelling, uplifting, and energizing. So, I ask again, what is YOUR vision for the future? Where do you want to see yourself in five years? Ten? What does your future look like to you? Have you thought about it? I'm sure you have, maybe in generalities but how about being specific? What is it that you would really like to do? What would you really like to accomplish? How about your organization? Where do you see it in five or ten years? What can you dream or imagine that if you could accomplish it would make all the difference in your life or in the life of your organization?

Mission Statements

During my tenure of teaching at the university I became enthralled with the power of mission statements. Much of what I was reading at the time focused on creating a mission statement that would inspire the workers to do greater things. During the 1990's many consultants made a great deal of money by taking the top people in a company on a retreat where they would "develop" a mission statement for their company. These executives would work hard creating, massaging and manipulating a bunch of words until they had THE mission statement for their company. They would then return to their company, maybe somewhat like Moses from the top of the mountain, with THE MISSION STATEMENT. They would often assemble their employees and have a big unveiling of a bronze plaque that would state what the mission of the company was and would extol all

"A clear vision, backed by definite plans, gives you a tremendous feeling of confidence and personal power."
Brian Tracy

employees to pay attention to the mission statement because it was going to lead them into the future. Unfortunately, that was where it ended for many of the companies. Occasionally, someone from the cleaning crew might read it as they were giving the plaque its monthly dusting, but other than that it basically went unnoticed. Employees were neither interested nor impassioned. Very few, if any, could remember the mission statement or even understand the part they played in achieving it. Many time in various classes, almost unanimously, students from many different types of organizations agreed that that was exactly what happened in their company. Once the plaque was unveiled, there was no continuing focus on the mission.

Mission statements, are important, I do not want to imply that they are not! Today, however, I have completely changed my thinking about the real importance of mission statements. I now realize that it is not the mission, but the vision that holds all the power. The mission statement is simply, or should be, a short, clear, concise statement that says why the organization exists. What is the purpose of the organization? Why are you sucking resources from this poor endangered planet?

 Whenever I would ask the students in my classes, "How many of you work for a company who has a mission statement?" almost everyone who worked raised their hands. I then told them, "Keep your hands up if you can tell me what that mission statement is," and virtually every hand would go down. Once in a great while, someone might be brave enough to give a half-hearted

"Our thoughts create our reality – where we put our focus is the direction we tend to go."

Peter McWilliams

attempt but would get lost in the endless verbiage. Only one time in ten years, did I have someone repeat their mission statement verbatim and go on to say that in their company, whenever a meeting was held, regardless of the reason, someone had to recite the mission statement without reading it. That was an organization I can imagine being led by a true leader. Mission statements help everyone stay focused on why they are there, why they are doing what they are doing, and why their work is important. One story that illustrates this is in "How Storytelling Can Keep Your Organization on Track" by Richard Stone:

"A long time ago an English gentleman was walking the streets of London, when he happened upon three workers laying stone. Curious about what they were building, he approached the first gentleman, tapped him on the shoulder, and asked, "What are you doing here?"

This first fellow hardly looked up as he slapped more mortar down, saying, "You must be blind if you can't see I'm laying stone."

Undeterred, the gentleman approached the second worker, and inquired about what he was working on. The second mason had little more to say. "Can't you see that I'm building a wall?"

Unwavering in his desire to find out what they were working on, our gentleman approached the third worker and asked him what he was building. This mason turned, stepped away from the wall, wiped off his hands, and

97

"For an athlete to function properly he must be intent, there has to be a definite purpose and goal in your progress. If you are not intent about what you are doing, you aren't able to resist the temptation to do something else that might be more fun at the moment."

John Wooden

said, "Why, I'm on the team that's building the cathedral to worship God!."

The Mission provides the why, the vision provides the where we are going. As I said before, it is the Vision that makes things happen, it is the vision that really holds the power, but even here, many organizations fall short. Whenever I would ask my students, "How many of you work for a company that has a vision statement?" a few hands would go up, however no one, not one single person could tell me what the vision of their company was! I find that to be really sad. The very people responsible for accomplishing the work of the organization have no idea where they are going, or why they are doing it! I will refer you back to the earlier quote about Alice in Wonderland. If you don't know where you are going, it really doesn't matter what road you take! It really doesn't matter where you are going or what you are doing! PERIOD! It is my judgment that the vast majority of workers today are totally unaware of what they are working toward and therefore their jobs become just that, a job, one in which they have little interest and one in which there is no fulfillment! They lose enthusiasm about what they are doing because they have no idea about where they are going, or the role they are playing in accomplishing something. There is no charted course! There is no passion and there is no interest in the job at hand.

Often, when I read a vision statement of a company, I feel that I am stuck in the mission statement time-warp! Again, it is full of beautiful, flowery words, and again,

"Focus more on your desire than your doubt and the dream will take care of itself . You may be surprised at how easily this happens. Your doubts are not as powerful as your desires, unless you make them so!"

Marcia Weider

often mentions something about 'enhancing shareholder value' –YUCK!! Also, many vision statements I see are very general, very generic in nature and scope, with no mention of time!

"We will become the best company in this industry, thereby enhancing our shareholders value by serving our customers to the best of our ability, driving success throughout all segments of our business, recognizing that our employees are our number one asset."

Does the above sound like a good vision statement to you? I'm hoping that you are saying NO, however based on what I have heard many times, many people do not see what is wrong with it. Well here is what I see wrong with it::

      1.   It is much too vague and non-specific. How do you know when you achieve the vision? How do you know when you become "best company in the industry" There are not standards of achievement!

      2.   There is no time-line. By when will it be accom-plished? If there is no completion time, where is the drive to make things happen now? Where is the urgency in what you are doing? In today's world, a company that does not have a sense of urgency, a real need to achieve a vision, will be left behind, lost in the dust of those companies moving ahead. We are living in a vastly different world, and companies in India

"Our deepest fear is not that we are inadequate. Our deepest fear is that we are powerful beyond measure. It is our light, not our darkness that most frightens us. We ask ourselves, who am I to be brilliant, gorgeous, talented fabulous? Actually, who are you not to be? You are a child of God. Your playing small doesn't serve the world. There's nothing enlightened about shrinking so that other people won't feel insecure around you. We were born to make manifest the glory of God that is within us. It's not just in some of us, it's in everyone. And as we let our own light shine, we unconsciously give other people permission to do the same. As we are liberated from our own fear, our presence automatically liberates others."
Marianne Williamson

and China are working very hard and are moving ahead and we need to catch up!

3.   So what? Although they are nice words, who cares? Are you inspired when you read your companies vision statement? If not, then it's time to find a new one!

4.   What specifically is it that you want to accomplish? Where are you going? Don't focus on the why, that is the purpose of the mission statement. Focus on your destination so that everyone in the organization has the sight set on the horizon.

5.   YAWN, pardon me, but I'm not too excited by it! Where's the passion? How I am supposed to really buy-in and want to work hard to accomplish something I am not excited about? Maybe, leader, you see the purpose, but if your employees don't buy into it you have a serious problem!

How about this one:

Within 5 years we will improve our customer satisfaction ratings to the point that 99%, or better, of our customers rate us as the best company to do business with, based on customer satisfaction surveys.

OR

Within 10 years, we will be the number one supplier of highest quality parts to the aerospace industry, based on number of parts supplied, dollar value of those parts and

"Without passion man is a mere latent force and possibility, like the flint which awaits the shock of the iron before it can give forth its spark."
Amiel, *Journal*, 17 December 1856

with the highest customer satisfaction rating of any company in the industry.

Both of these statements are much more precise, clearly stating what will be achieved and by when. Benchmarks! In order to get excited about working toward achieving a vision, we need to know how achievement is going to be measured, and how much time we have to achieve the vision. We need to be able to monitor our progress. Imagine taking a road trip and never having any idea of where you are, how far you have driven, and no idea at all of how long it is going to get to where you want to go! Sounds like a fun trip, doesn't it!

There is absolutely nothing wrong with dreaming big, for only great things are achieved by those who dare to dream big! I often get asked, "Well, what if we don't achieve that? What if we fall short?" My response: "If you do fall short and do not achieve the vision, will you be better off or worse off than you would be if you didn't even attempt to achieve the vision?

A case in point: Some time back, I had a meeting with, John, who was a regional vice-president for one of the nation's largest banks. He was in charge of Customer Development for a 7-State region. During our conversation I asked, "What is your vision for you part of your organization?" "Huh?" he responded. "What do you want your organization to accomplish in the future?" "Well," he responded, "I want to continue to do well. We currently increase our customer base by 3% to 4%

"You don't have to be a fantastic hero to do certain things – to compete. You can be just an ordinary chap sufficiently motivated to reach challenging goals."
Sir Edmund Hillary

each year and that is pretty good." I then asked him, "What if you were to tell your staff that your vision was to increase your customer base by 50% within 5 years?" I was very surprised by his response. He actually jumped, as though I had hit him and looked at me incredulously. "Are you serious?" he almost yelled. He looked as though he was very shocked by such a proposal. "What's wrong," I asked, "Is that not possible?" "Well," he replied, "It's possible, I guess, but I don't know..." as his voice trailed off. When I followed up with another question, he did not want to talk about it any longer and moved on to another subject.

So what if he set this considerable increase as his vision and they fall short and only increased their customer base by 40% or even 30%?. Did they fail? I don't believe so, not by a long shot! If their current growth rate was 2-3% a year, at best in 5 years they would have a 15% growth rate versus a 30% or 40% growth rate by clearly stating the vision and getting everyone behind it and working hard. So, again, would it have been considered that they failed because they did not achieve the vision? Maybe, by some people's standards, but certainly not by mine! A huge part of the past way of managing in many organizations was from a negative approach. Looking for what is wrong and treating "failures" or even mistakes in a highly responsive and negative way has created fear throughout organizations. It has created a sense of not wanting to step out of the comfort zone and try something new. In many organizations the majority of employees are sitting and waiting to be told what to do and how to do it because that is how it has been for

"Never look down to test the ground before taking your next step; only he who keeps his eye fixed on the far horizon will find the right road"

Dag Hammarsjkold

decades and we can no longer afford to work this way.

Of course, just having a vision and being able to communicate that vision is not enough to make it happen. The real Leader has to be constantly involved, encouraging, coaching, motivating and leading his/her followers to always working toward achieving the vision and removing obstacles in their path. Leaders, like parents, must be willing to accept mistakes and failings as part of growing and learning. Employees must know that their best interest in first and foremost in the minds of the leaders and that it is okay to make a mistake. The followers must know why achieving the vision is important, why it is a 'burning platform' so to speak, and specifically what role they are playing in achieving that vision, Ultimately, they need to know what is in it for them if the vision is achieved. I do not know very many people who are willing to really work hard and put in extra effort simply to "enhance shareholder value," do you? What is the meaningful, tangible result the workers will realize if the vision is achieved? Everyone needs to be encouraged, supported, and feel that what they do truly matters to their leaders and to the organization itself.

If the vision is to increase the profit margin by X%, maybe some of that increase should be returned to the workers! I often tell those who participate in my classes

"Focus on your potential,
instead of your limitations."
Alan Loy McGinnis

that we all listen to the same radio station, 24/7! There isn't anyone, anywhere that doesn't listen to this radio station because it drives everything we do! What is that station?

WII-FM
(What's In It For Me!)

I'll have more to say about this later, when I cover the topic of the importance of a Leader really knowing and understanding him/herself and why he/she does the things he/she does. To truly know yourself, and what motivates you, and why you do the things you do, gives amazing insight into what motivates others. We all work with our own self-interest in mind.

Final Thoughts on Vision

Sometime during the 1970's, while I was working a rotating shift, I was home during the day and happened to be watching television when I heard that Ray Kroc, the CEO and founder of one of the world's largest fast-food empires, McDonalds, was to be the guest on the Phil Donahue show. I found Mr. Kroc to be extremely interesting and I wanted to hear what he had to say. During the conversation, as Kroc was extolling the virtue and the importance of cleanliness, value and the ability of customers knowing that they could go into a McDonalds anywhere in the world and expect the same experience and how important those things were to the future of the company. He said that every McDonalds

"*Don't underestimate the power of a vision. McDonald's founder, Ray Kroc, pictured his empire long before it existed, and he saw how to get there. He invented the company motto —
'Quality, service, cleanliness and value' — and kept repeating it to employees for the rest of his life.*"

Kenneth Labich

manager knew that his/her main job was to main the highest standards possible. Kroc explained that it was the customers' expectations that were driving the success of his company and if the customers found that they could not rely on the things he said they could expect, regardless of the restaurant's location, then the business would not survive. As the conversation continued, Kroc talked about whenever he was on the road he would stop at a McDonald's restaurant to check it out. Since few people recognized him, he was able to check out the service, quality and cleanliness of the place without people knowing who he was.

At this point, Donahue asked Kroc, "Well, so what would you do if you went into a restaurant and found that the restroom was not as clean as you have said it would be?" Without hesitation, Kroc responded emphatically, "That's easy, I would go get me a mop and a bucket and I would go clean the restroom!" Somewhat incredulous, Donahue replied, "Oh come on, Ray, are you telling me that as one of the richest men in America you would actually clean a restroom yourself?" "Absolutely, I would," Kroc responded, "Because my word is what my customers rely on and I have promised my customers that cleanliness is something they will find when they enter a McDonalds, so I would definitely clean the bathroom. Then I would go find out why it was dirty in the first place!" With that, there was not mistake that Ray Kroc was a man of his word, a man who had a clear vision of what he wanted to create, and a man who held himself and his employees to very high and exacting standards. I also felt as though he was a man I did not want to let

*"Capital isn't scarce,
vision is"*
Sam Walton

down if I was an employee!   Kroc also knew and understood that having a vision wasn't enough.   He understood that as the leader of a world-wide empire he had to continuously state his vision and what he expected. He knew that he could not just rely on those who reported to him to get the message out and that it was his job to make sure that everyone in the organization knew his standards. His ability to clearly communicate what he so clearly saw, enabled McDonald's to rapidly grow and remain focused on the core points of Kroc's vision.

"Good business leaders create a vision, articulate the vision, passionately own the vision, and relentlessly drive it to completion."
Jack Welch

CHAPTER THREE

INTEGRITY

[3: the quality or state of being complete or undivided: Completeness]

A Leader who does not practice integrity is a leader of chaos!

For most people, when they hear the word integrity, they think about morals and ethics, and certainly, this is important. Lack of moral integrity has probably driven most of the failures in our economic system in one way or another. However, I choose to use the word integrity for a totally different purpose. Integrity, in this instance, means a consistent behavior that is focused on achieving the vision without distraction or going off in a different direction. The definition above is important for our discussion about Leadership as I believe a Leader must stay focused in a complete and undivided way if he/she wants to accomplish the vision he/she has in mind. So often I have seen, or talked to different people, who tell me about their vision, goals, objectives, etc. and how important they are to them. When I ask them to tell me about some of the things they are doing or projects they are working on, they often begin telling me about something that is not even remotely connected to their Vision, or is actually working in the opposite direction. When questioned about the discrepancy, they will most often say, "Well I am still working on accomplishing the

"Upon the conduct of each depends the fate of all."
Alexander The Great

vision but this is important too," and it may well be, however if it is not aligned specifically with the vision, then it is taking valuable time, resources and energy away from the vision itself. Also, I have seen organizations in which different employees, or even whole departments, are given opposing goals to achieve, often neither of which are in alignment with the vision! When employees and departments are in competition for money or other resources, the only outcome possible is chaos and non-achievement of the vision.

As a training consultant, I often get very quizzical looks when I tell my clients, "Stop wasting your time, energy and other resources on training!" This obviously confuses them since I am there to talk about the training I can provide. I have been totally amazed at the number of companies that I have come across that offer many different training programs to their employees, which on the surface looks like a good thing, and it may be if the company has more money than they know what to do with and just want to offer some 'feel-good' training but has no specific application to the achievement of the vision. Training should be focused, vision-driven and competency based. I call this non-aligned training, "spaghetti-throwing training." If you were to take a handful of spaghetti and throw it against the wall, the largest part of it is going to fall off, land on the floor and get walked on. Some of it will stick, only to fall off later, and a very small part of it will actually become a part of the wall itself. Spaghetti-throwing training is training that is not backed up within the organization, not re-enforced by any actions of the hierarchy, nor does it have

"Leadership is practiced not so much in words as in attitude and in actions."

Harold Geneen

anything to do in enhancing the skills necessary to achieve the vision. I'll give you an example. Many years ago, when I first became a supervisor with one company I worked for, I was sent to Basic Supervision training. This training lasted for five full days and was an off-the-shelf training program that was purchased at a rather high cost from a recognized training consulting company.

Don't get me wrong, the training offered some very good ideas in working with people, managing work flow, etc., etc., however, the only time I heard about any of the practices I was taught, was during the 5 days I spent in class! Even worse, in the many years I continued to work with this company, I never saw anyone in management practicing any of the communication or employee relations tools I was taught. Worse yet, when someone was promoted to a Manager's position, they were sent to the second-level course and again, there was never any mention or observable actions that anything taught in the course were actually used. Why? Why would a company spend such a great deal of money and time and not work to get the most bang for the buck? I believe it was a lack of focus and a lack of integrity to what they wanted to accomplish.

If a Leader is practicing integrity, the vision would be the driving force for everything that gets done in the organization, especially in training the employees responsible for accomplishing the vision. As in everything else in leadership, IT STARTS AT THE TOP! Everything that happens in an organization, EVERYHING, is a direct result of the leadership in the

"Goals provide the energy source that powers our lives. One of the best ways we can get the most from the energy we have is to focus it. That is what goals can do for us; concentrate our energy."

Dennis Whatley

organization. Training is the #1 area that gets built up when times are good and the first area to get cut when times are lean. I believe that it should always be the last to be cut! I know, I know, you are thinking, "Of course you would say that, you're a training consultant," but that is not the reason I say that. In lean time, training the work force in the skills necessary to accomplish the vision is even more critical than ever before. In lean times it is essential that every member of the organization is at the top to their game and able to perform to the best of their ability.

Whenever an individual's supervisor wants that employee to attend a particular training, that supervisor should sit down with the employee and talk about the training, what they should expect to cover and what the supervisor specifically wants the employee to focus on learning, why it is important, and how it will help the employee in achieving their part of the vision. Also, within a very short time frame after the training is over the two should sit down again and the supervisor should seek to learn from the employee what he/she learned, what three to five specific things he/she is going to do to effectively integrate what was learned as a result of the training and what, specifically, the supervisor can do to assist the employee in making those improvements a part of their everyday job. Together they should write specific and measurable goals based on the outcomes they intend to see. The evaluation of these goals can then be used in performance management, which should be a joint endeavor. Many think that performance management is an opportunity to tell the employee what he/she did NOT

"It is during our darkest moments that we must focus to see the light."
Aristotle

accomplish and that is the completely wrong approach. Performance management is an opportunity for a supervisor to act as a mentor and coach and assist the employee in discovering what worked and how they can build more of what worked into their daily efforts. It should be an opportunity for a leader to assist the employee in discovering for him or herself what they want to work on improving. Now, of course, this would mean that the supervisor would have to know and understand the concepts that were taught in the training the employee attended and actually be demonstrating those concepts on a daily basis! In all cases, actions speak louder than words and if an employee is being taught one thing but sees just the opposite being applied every day on the job then what was learned in training will be for naught!

To accomplish a vision, there must be complete, constant and directed focus on achieving that vision. There needs to be a complete focus and constancy of purpose throughout the organization, starting at the top and reaching all the way through the organization. Every employee must be fully engaged and mindful of the role he/she plays in accomplishing the vision. If someone were to go up to an employee and ask, "What is it that you are doing, specifically, that helps drive this organization to the accomplishment of the vision?" The answer must be clear, specific and mindful. It must be unequivocal. In today's business world, there can be no half hearted awareness or focus on the part of any employee.

"Our goals can only be reached through a vehicle of a plan, in which we must fervently believe, and upon which we must vigorously act. There is no other route to success."

Stephen A. Brennan

If great things are to be accomplished, then great things must be expected from everyone! By far, the majority of employees I have encountered throughout my working life, have wanted to accomplish great things. Employees want to be a part of something greater than themselves. They want to be a part of an organization that strives to include the totality of who they are in the growth and success of the business. Sadly, many leaders today do not know how to accomplish this. Or maybe that it is they do not believe the employees are truly capable of For most people, when they hear the word integrity, they think about morals and ethics, and certainly, this is important. Lack of moral integrity has probably driven most of the failures in our economic system in one way or another. However, I choose to use the word integrity for a totally different purpose. Integrity, in this instance, means a consistent behavior that is focused on achieving the vision without distraction or going off in a different direction. The definition above is important for our discussion about Leadership as I believe a Leader must stay focused in a complete and undivided way if he/she wants to accomplish the vision he/she has in mind. So often I have seen, or talked to different people, who tell me about their vision, goals, objectives, etc. and how important they are to them. When I ask them to tell me about some of the things they are doing or projects they are working on, they often begin telling me about something that is not even remotely connected to their Vision, or is actually working in the opposite direction. When questioned about the discrepancy, they will most often say, "Well I am still working on accomplishing the vision but this is important too," and it may well be,

"A visionary company doesn't simply balance between idealism and profitability; it seeks to be highly idealistic and highly profitable. A visionary company doesn't simply balance between preserving a tightly held core ideology and stimulating vigorous change and movement, it does both to an extreme"

Jim Collins

however if it is not aligned specifically with the vision, then it is taking valuable time, resources and energy away from the vision itself. Also, I have seen organizations in which different employees, or even whole departments, are given opposing goals to achieve, often neither of which are in alignment with the vision! When employees and departments are in competition for money or other resources, the only outcome possible is chaos and non-achievement of the vision.

As a training consultant, I often get very quizzical looks when I tell my clients, "Stop wasting your time, energy and other resources on training!" This obviously confuses them since I am there to talk about the training I can provide. I have been totally amazed at the number of companies that I have come across that offer many different training programs to their employees, which on the surface looks like a good thing, and it may be if the company has more money than they know what to do with and just want to offer some 'feel-good' training but has no specific application to the achievement of the vision. Training should be focused, vision-driven and competency based. I call this non-aligned training, "spaghetti-throwing training." If you were to take a handful of spaghetti and throw it against the wall, the largest part of it is going to fall off, land on the floor and get walked on. Some of it will stick, only to fall off later, and a very small part of it will actually become a part of the wall itself. Spaghetti-throwing training is training that is not backed up within the organization, not re-enforced by any actions of the hierarchy, nor does it have

"A leader's role is to raise people's aspirations for what they can become and to release their energies so they will try to get there."

David Gergen

anything to do in enhancing the skills necessary to achieve the vision. I'll give you an example. Many years ago, when I first became a supervisor with one company I worked for, I was sent to Basic Supervision training. This training lasted for five full days and was an off-the-shelf training program that was purchased at a rather high cost from a recognized training consulting company.

Don't get me wrong, the training offered some very good ideas in working with people, managing work flow, etc., etc., however, the only time I heard about any of the practices I was taught, was during the 5 days I spent in class! Even worse, in the many years I continued to work with this company, I never saw anyone in organization, especially management practicing any of the communication or employee relations tools I was taught. Worse yet, when someone was promoted to a Manager's position, they were sent to the second-level course and again, there was never any mention or observable actions that anything taught in the course were actually used. Why? Why would a company spend such a great deal of money and time and not work to get the most bang for the buck? I believe it was a lack of focus and a lack of integrity to what they wanted to accomplish.

If a Leader is practicing integrity, the vision would be the driving force for everything that gets done in the responsible for accomplishing the vision. As in everything else in leadership, IT STARTS AT THE TOP! Everything that happens in an organization, EVERYHING, is a direct result of the leadership in the

131

"The secret of success is constancy of purpose."
Benjamin Disraeli

organization. Training is the #1 area that gets built up when times are good and the first area to get cut when times are lean. I believe that it should always be the last to be cut! I know, I know, you are thinking, "Of course you would say that, you're a training consultant," but that is not the reason I say that. In lean time, training the work force in the skills necessary to accomplish the vision is even more critical than ever before. In lean times it is essential that every member of the organization is at the top to their game and able to perform to the best of their ability.

Whenever an individual's supervisor wants that employee to attend a particular training, that supervisor should sit down with the employee and talk about the training, what they should expect to cover and what the supervisor specifically wants the employee to focus on learning, why it is important, and how it will help the employee in achieving their part of the vision. Also, within a very short time frame after the training is over the two should sit down again and the supervisor should seek to learn from the employee what he/she learned, what three to five specific things he/she is going to do to effectively integrate what was learned as a result of the training and what, specifically, the supervisor can do to assist the employee in making those improvements a part of their everyday job. Together they should write specific and measurable goals based on the outcomes they intend to see. The evaluation of these goals can then be used in performance management, which should be a joint endeavor. Many think that performance management is an opportunity to tell the employee what he/she did NOT

"Integrity is the essence of everything successful."
Richard Buckminster

accomplish and that is the completely wrong approach. Performance management is an opportunity for a supervisor to act as a mentor and coach and assist the employee in discovering what worked and how they can build more of what worked into their daily efforts. It should be an opportunity for a leader to assist the employee in discovering for him or herself what they want to work on improving. Now, of course, this would mean that the supervisor would have to know and understand the concepts that were taught in the training the employee attended and actually be demonstrating those concepts on a daily basis! In all cases, actions speak louder than words and if an employee is being taught one thing but sees just the opposite being applied every day on the job then what was learned in training will be for naught!

To accomplish a vision, there must be complete, constant and directed focus on achieving that vision. There needs to be a complete focus and constancy of purpose throughout the organization, starting at the top and reaching all the way through the organization. Every employee must be fully engaged and mindful of the role he/she plays in accomplishing the vision. If someone were to go up to an employee and ask, "What is it that you are doing, specifically, that helps drive this organization to the accomplishment of the vision?" The answer must be clear, specific and mindful. It must be unequivocal. In today's business world, there can be no half hearted awareness or focus on the part of any employee.

"One reason so few of us achieve what we truly want is that we never direct our focus; we never concentrate our power. Most people dabble their way through life, never deciding to master anything in particular."
Tony Robbins

If great things are to be accomplished, then great things must be expected from everyone! By far, the majority of employees I have encountered throughout my working life, have wanted to accomplish great things. Employees want to be a part of something greater than themselves. They want to be a part of an organization that strives to include the totality of who they are in the growth and success of the business. Sadly, many leaders today do not know how to accomplish this. Or maybe that it is they do not believe the employees are truly capable of doing more than they are being allowed to do, which is a carryover from the top-down, hierarchical approach to leadership. Of course, there is the possibility that there are those employees who aren't interested in being a part of the organization and its success and if they exist, it is a very small minority, but sadly, all employees are treated as if they are this type of employee! If there is a terminally unhappy employee who does not respond to coaching and mentoring then they need to be encouraged to move on to an organization in which they might feel more comfortable and be more willing to contribute to that organization's success. As Jim Collins stated in *"From Good to Great"* not every employee is on the right seat on the bus and occasionally an employee is even on the wrong bus and the leader's job is to help each employee find the right bus to be on and the right seat to sit in within their organization. My belief is that employees who are disengaged and not a team player are that way as a result of being sidelined and not listened to for so long that their motivation and passion have grown dim.

"The key to success is to focus our conscious mind on things we desire not things we fear."
Brian Tracy

Many years ago, early in my management career, I was selected to be the Lead Facilitator for a large scale management change effort. The electric utility I worked for at the time was moving out of the dark ages and wanted to get employees more involved by implementing a Total Quality employee involvement effort. As the Lead Facilitator, I began going to each of the 7 districts I was responsible, traveling to 3 different states, meeting with the District Manager and his staff, to explain the process by which we would begin the implementation of this massive effort. Now keep in mind, this was a completely new way of doing things, and not every Manager was thrilled about the idea which made my efforts that much more difficult! I remember one particular district I went to where there was a great deal of skepticism by the entire management staff. The more I worked to explain the process of selecting volunteer employee teams, conducting the training, and holding weekly meetings so the employees could work on solving their own problems, the more skeptical the staff seemed to be. At one point, the more I explained the process the more two supervisors in the back corner of the room would whisper to each other and laugh. I finally stopped and asked them if they had some concerns about what we were going to do, and one of them spoke up and said, "Yeah, we want to wait and see what happens when you meet, Bill!" With that, the entire room began laughing. "What about, Bill?" I asked. Everyone began explaining that Bill was their number one problem child. Bill, it seemed, never had anything good to say about anything and was a real thorn in everyone's side.

"Most people have no idea of the giant capacity we can immediately command when we focus all of our resources on mastering a single area of our lives."

Tony Robbins

After this meeting, I held a meeting in the afternoon with all employees in the district. There was a ripple of excitement, as well as a great deal of skepticism as they had never been given an opportunity to work on their own problems, or even had the option to voice their opinions openly. After I completed the presentation, there were several questions about the mechanics of how the process would work but generally, it was very positive and upbeat. I explained that the first team would be selected from a group of volunteers and if there were more who wanted to be on the team than the 8 to 10 we were looking for, we would draw names out of a hat. After the meeting adjourned and I was beginning to collect my material, I turned and found I was face to face with a man who said, "I have a question! Who's going to draw the names out of the hat?" I was a bit perplexed as that was a question I had not contemplated. "Well," I responded, "I'm not sure who will do it, why do you ask?" "Well, I just figure that there will be some names taped to the bottom of the hat so they can't be drawn!" he responded rather emphatically! I looked him in the eye and said, "Well, I can promise you that is not going to happen, in fact, I now know who will draw the names." You have probably guessed by now, that the person I was talking to was, Bill! "Yeah, who?" Bill asked. "You are," I responded. "No way, not me," Bill stated, to which I told him that if he did not draw the names, then I was moving on to another district and we would not be starting a team there for a while. Well, Bill did draw the names and the last name he drew out of the hat was, you guessed it, his!

"We can always choose to perceive things differently. You can focus on what's wrong in your life, or you can focus on what's right."
Marianne Williamson

Bill turned out to be one of the best team members of any team I had the great fortune to work with. He worked hard, had a lot of great ideas and was a great motivator to the other team members. Bill was also the district's union shop steward which went a long way to getting other employees on board.

So how could this 'problem child', this person that every member of the management team saw as an obstacle to getting things done, turn out to be one of the best and most engaged team members? I believe it was that Bill finally had an outlet for his ideas and his enthusiasm and his passion for seeing things improve. He was able to make a connection between what he was doing every day and something greater that could be accomplished. As it turned out, Bill also owned his own business. He was a martial arts instructor and from what I heard he was very good at it. Over the years, as I began observing employees in many different organizations I found that a great number of 'low-level' employees owned their own businesses, chaired committees or social or church groups, or were leaders in some other capacity, however when they walked through the doors of the company they worked for they were considered to be unable to do the tasks they were doing outside of work. The leader's role in each and every organization is to constantly provide managing its employees with a decidedly dictatorial approach. I had a conversation with one employee who was operating a very large milling machine on which a computer was cutting a rather large part from a huge slab of titanium. This slab of titanium was approximately three feet thick by 15 feet wide by 30 feet long. A very

"Don't dwell on what went wrong. Instead, focus on what to do next. Spend your energies on moving forward toward finding the answer."
Dennis Waitley

the connection between what people do every day and where the organization is going. It is to tap into the creativity, talent and abilities of each employee and allow them to be fully engaged, heart, mind and soul. By allowing each employee to be fully engaged a great storehouse of energy is released and great things begin to happen. It is imperative that the integrity of the vision be maintained each and every day so that everyone fully understands and remembers why they are doing what they are doing!

I once worked for a brief period of time with an aerospace manufacturing company that had a history of expensive process to say the least! As I walked by I could see that the machine operator was rather upset and so I stopped to see what the problem was. He told me that the computer program was wrong and the part was going to have to be scrapped because it would come out wrong. I asked him if he had told his supervisor about the problem and he indicated that he had and was told that it wasn't his concern and he should continue to run the part as instructed. He was told that the engineering department sent the computer program to the machine and it wasn't their place to question it! How much money might a slab of titanium this size cost? Obviously there was a major defect, not just in the computer programming, but in programming of the employees within the organization!

This is a great example of a company not working in integrity with its mission or vision. Often, it seems that departments within an organization function from totally

"I can't change the direction of the wind, but I can adjust my sails to always reach my destination."

Jimmy Dean

different goals and directions which can run counter to run another. Who benefits from this kind of nonsense? Not the employees because they can see what is going on and over time withdraw their enthusiasm and passion for the job, and become somewhat angry because they feel their efforts are being wasted. Certainly the company is not benefitting because it leads to increased costs, lack of production and low worker morale. AND this is certainly no way to 'enhance shareholder value!'

On my last day working with this company, I seriously considered getting the largest cardboard box I could find and placing it by the employee's entrance with a sign above it that read, "Please deposit your brains and your hearts here, as neither are needed inside. You may pick them up on your way home!"

Now you may think that the story of the wrongly produced part was ridiculous, which it was, and you may also be thinking that this sort of thing does not happen very often or in too many organizations, but based on many conversations I have had with employees in many different companies, is that situations like this happen all the time. Where in your organization does this occur? Are there elements of this occurring? If you say, "Absolutely not!" are you sure? How do you know? I bet if I were to ask your employees I am sure that I would quite possibly would here some interesting stories!

In many of my MBA classes I have conducted an exercise entitled "Win as Much as You Can" which highlights the situation of departments fighting against

"The more intensely we feel about an idea or a goal, the more assuredly the idea, buried deep in our subconscious, will direct us along the path to its fulfillment."

Earl Nightingale

one another in order to 'win', often at the cost of the entire company. This is a very dramatic exercise that has far reaching implications. I would often assign the class to write a 5-page paper based on this exercise and I would get papers full of horror stories of what they had experienced similar to this exercise within their own companies. Many times I received papers that were extremely self-reflective where students would recognize parts of themselves that they were shocked to find.

Many of the papers spoke of recognizing greed, vindictiveness, and a strong sense that the end justifies any means. Some students took the exercise lightly and put little thought into it, but far more found it to be a real eye opener and several vowed that they were going to use that exercise as a guide to their own ethical conduct!

Integrity, a true and constant focus on what it is you want and specific goals that mesh and blend together seamlessly so that the power of the entire organization is focused in one direction. It is critical in the drive to success. In today's economy, no organization can afford to go helter-skelter in many different directions with no true direction in mind. Everyone in the organization needs to clearly know where they are going, why it is important, and that everyone in the entire organization is pulling together in the same direction.

Integrity is every employee or member of the organization knowing very specifically their role in accomplishing the Vision and working with great

"Only as high as I reach can I grow, only as far as I seek can I go, only as deep as I look can I see, only as much as I dream can I be."

Karen Ravn

enthusiasm and passion toward achieving that vision. This enthusiasm and Passion is a product of their leader's own enthusiasm and Passion of which they are reminded every single day. The Leader MUST demonstrate this enthusiasm and Passion with never ending focus on the horizon. The Leader plays many roles and one of the most important is salesperson for the Vision. The Leader is completely responsible for the results of the organization. The Leader might be able to delegate projects, tasks and authority but the one thing a Leader cannot delegate is accountability! Especially when it comes to Vision, Integrity and Passion!

If you want to achieve great things, then you must be able and willing to think big things. You must be willing to allow yourself and others the opportunity to dream, to imagine, to think of what could be rather than what is. See in your mind that which you want to see with your eyes! In the words of Mahatma Gandhi, "Be the change you want to see!" Small dreams produce small results and organizations today cannot afford small results if they want to be successful. Integrity is also about setting very specific, measurable, achievable, realistic and time-based goals. Without each of these specifics, your goals are nothing more than 'I wants' and not I will do's! I was prepared to write about a Harvard Business School study on goal-setting. The study, as the story went told about a graduating class who was asked how many had actual goals of where they wanted to go in life and what they wanted to accomplish and if those goals were written down with a specific end-date. Supposedly, only 3% of the class had such goals, and when the researchers con-

"Any person who selects a goal in life which can be fully achieved, has already defined his own limitations"

Cavett Robert

tacted members of that graduating class twenty years later they found that the 3% with goals had over 10 times the accumulated wealth of the remaining 97% of the class combined. This study seemed to be rather staggering, however there is one flaw. It seems that the story is bogus! An urban myth! There seems to be no supporting evidence of this particular study.

However, a study was conducted at Dominican University. Participants were divided into five different groups:

Group 1: Participants were asked to think about something they wanted to accomplish over the next 4 weeks.

Group 2: Participants were asked to write their goals down, or in the case of the study to type their goals into the study survey.

Group 3: Participants were asked to not only write their goals but also to formulate some action commitments.

Group 4: Participants were asked to not only complete the actions of the participants in Group 3 but to also send their goals and their commitments to a supportive friend.

Group 5: Participants were asked to do everything Group 4 was asked to do but also commit to sending a weekly progress report to their friend.

"What we see depends mainly on what we look for."

John Lubbock

The end results showed that all groups with written goals had a higher mean goal achievement than those who did not write their goals and, not surprisingly, the group that had the highest mean achievement was Group 5 that not only wrote down their goals but also committed to taking specific actions and then following up with weekly progress reports.

Clearly, to achieve your Vision, rather it be large or small, involving an entire organization or just yourself, aligning your actions with very clear specific goals and aligning your organization to accomplishing those goals so that everyone is working in integrity to the vision is a vital ingredient to success.

"The greater the loyalty of a group toward the group, the greater is the motivation among the members to achieve the goals of the group, and the greater the probability that the group will achieve its goals."

Rensis Likert

CHAPTER FOUR

PASSION

[4 a (1): emotion *<his ruling passion is greed> (2)plural : the emotions as distinguished from reason b: intense, driving, or overmastering feeling or conviction]*

A Leader without passion has no followers!

Passion is the fire that burns deep in your heart, your soul and in the very depth of who and what you are. It is the drive that moves each of us towards something that is critical to us. It is that ever-driving need to achieve something, to acquire something, to be something. Passion stirs the emotions and drives each of us forward. Passion is responsible for all that has ever been accomplished in human history. It is the drive for something better, something new, something unknowing, the need to reach greater heights.

Passion is the intense desire to reach a new plateau. It was passion that drove the early settlers of the New World westward: passion for freedom, for a new life, for something different. It was passion for beating the Soviets in the arms race that created the drive for achieving the vision of putting a man on the moon and returning him to earth safely. It was also passion that drove a diminutive Nun to spend the majority of her life working in the slums of Calcutta, India caring, supporting and loving the people who were the lowest of

"Our passions are the winds that propel our vessel. Our reason is the pilot that steers her. Without winds the vessel would not move, and without a pilot she would be lost."

Proverb

the low in Indian society and in the greatest need of help.

Passion is the single underlying emotion that has driven man to success, as well as failure. Passion can be either for something good or something bad. Hitler was certainly a leader who had great passion for his cause, albeit a cause without a sense of morality in the world view. The underlying motivators are what are important, however as Hitler so aptly proved, a leader with a Vision, moral or not, the Integrity to focus all efforts toward accomplishing that Vision, and a deep and unending Passion that drives him and his followers forward can accomplish a great deal.

I'm certain that every single human being has experienced great passion at some point in his/her life. Either the immense passion felt in a sexual encounter, or the intense need for something tangible or intangible. We have all felt that deep inner drive to achieve or accomplish something. I remember when I was young, 13 or 14, I had a paper route and one day I was told that there would be a contest, and I was given a catalog from which I could choose a wide variety of prizes. The prizes would be awarded depending on the number of magazine subscriptions we sold. The higher number of subscriptions sold, the greater the prize. One of the top prizes, was a portable typewriter. Although this may seem like an unlikely choice of a 13 year old boy, at that time, I had a deep passion to go to college after graduating from high school. For whatever reason, I saw that typewriter as a tool I could use to succeed in college. However, it took a large number of magazine sales to

"If there is no passion in your life, then have you really lived? Find your passion, whatever it may be. Become it, let it become you and you will find great things happen FOR you, TO you and BECAUSE of you!"

T. Alan Armstrong

achieve this great prize. The town in which I grew up was a very small town, with a population of only 311 people, and I delivered a daily paper to approximately 50+ homes, so I was uncertain how I was going to be able to sell enough subscriptions to meet my goal.

The passion I had at that time to achieve my goal was my greatest asset. It drove me forward and I was able to talk to people with a sense of heightened focus which helped me achieve my goal. In fact, I was told I sold more subscriptions that many in areas with much larger routes. Passion, regardless of the desired result, regardless of where it is you want to go, will help drive you to success. In fact, Passion is the ONLY thing that will keep you going when times get rough. During those times when all things look lost, when the dark days seem endless, your Passion for what you want to accomplish will keep driving you forward.

There is a great story about Thomas Edison and his work on inventing the light bulb. Time after time, Edison tried a different substance for the filament of the bulb and time after time he failed to achieve what he KNEW was achievable. His passion for accomplishing what he KNEW in his heart kept driving him forward, and again, time after time he failed. Much was written about his failures and many people were beginning to laugh at this man who was continuing to fail at something everyone else knew was impossible. At one point, when asked about his many failures, Edison supposedly replied that he was, "failing his way to success." By the time he achieved success, he had tried over two thousand

"A strong passion for any object will ensure success, for the desire for the end will point out the means."

William Hazlitt

different substances to use as a filament! Success to Edison was something he KNEW in his heart was simply a matter of finding the right element. He did not let temporary setbacks get in his way!

How do we "get" passion for something, especially in business? What if there is something that we can readily agree would really be great to achieve but we really aren't sure we can do it, or just aren't sure we want to go through the hassle, or the hard work to get there? Just like the Sr. Vice President of a bank I talked about in the chapter on Vision, he agreed that it would be great to increase the customer base by 50% in 5 years but he wasn't sure it could be done and he wasn't sure he wanted to go through the work necessary to achieve success. Well, if you as the leader has doubts, guess what, your followers will have greater doubts and your goal will NOT be achieved. You as the leader have to demonstrate the confidence in your Vision, you have to continually make sure that you have Integrity throughout your organization and that it is not only aligned, but completely focused on achieving the Vision. AND you have to show that you have Passion for the Vision, that you CARE about going the distance.

My most favorite movie of all time is Field of Dreams. This movie has many messages on many different important levels that touch our hearts and stir feelings deep within. I believe it touched the hearts of so many people because its underlying message was about passion for a dream, even if we do not fully understand the dream. It spoke to the center of who we are, about

"When work, commitment, and pleasure all become one and you reach that deep well where passion lives, nothing is impossible!"
Unknown

believing in something greater than ourselves, about having the passion to do something that at times may not make sense to others, and that by having a deep, unyielding passion that we remain so totally focused on, we can maybe, just maybe, accomplish the impossible!

One of the most memorable mantras of the movie, of course, is "If you build it he will come!" This line has been recycled in ads across the spectrum, but it speaks to achieving the impossible, it speaks to that part of each of us to do something extraordinary. A second memorable line that I believe really speaks more clearly to our discussion here is, "Go the distance!" Do not give up! Just like Edison having a belief in what he was doing that was so strong that it carried him through countless failed attempts at success. "Go the distance!" Maintain your Vision! Maintain that Integrity throughout your organization, and most importantly maintain your Passion!

Of course, in business we cannot allow ourselves to become hopelessly lost in achieving a Vision simply for the sake of achieving the Vision. We must be accountable for our actions to the success of the organization. An inevitable fact of life, for many in business, is that they have someone else to whom they are accountable. Even the independent entrepreneur is accountable to those he/she owes money to, his/her family to maintain their lifestyle, etc.

An unyielding fact of life in today's world is that things change. Change is occurring in every aspect of our lives

"Chase down your passion like it's the last bus of the night."
Glade Byron Addams

and although change has been occurring for eons, it seems to be occurring more rapidly today than at any other time in history. There are those who say that time is actually accelerating and therefore change is indeed occurring more rapidly. Although I find the thought and the concept proposed by the ancient Mayans to be very intriguing, I'm not convinced that they were right. However, what is right is that we must constantly and continually deal with the effects of change in our lives. Many people have said, but what if things change? What if I no longer want to do that, or what if the business environment changes and we can no longer continue to work toward the Vision we thought we wanted? What if my Passion has changed, for whatever reason? What if, what if, what if......?

Well, what do you think? What would you do? Would you continue to work blindly toward a vision that has been rendered ineffective due to changes in the business environment? Of course not! You would change course, you would change the Vision to meet the changes you are experiencing along the way. Having a Vision does not mean that you are committed no matter what, but you must be careful, you must make sure that you are not giving up on your Vision simply because things are getting difficult. Some questions you might want to ask yourself, or others in your organization are:

1. Can this Vision still be achieved?
2. Would achieving this Vision still be beneficial to our organization?

"Follow your passion, and success will follow you."
Arthur Buddhold

3. What things have changed in our business environment that might impact this Vision?
4. Do we still have the Passion to achieve this Vision? If not, why not? What has changed?
5. Do we need to tweak, or change the Vision completely to better serve the organization?

You may find, that you still have the Passion; however the climate has changed to the extent that it makes the Vision no longer viable. It is very difficult to give up on a dream, especially if you still have a great deal of passion for the dream. Again, I think the previous questions would apply to your passion just as well. Is it possible to channel that passion toward a Vision that is more achievable? Can your passion still be the fuel that drives your organization forward to success?

One last thing about passion: YOU, Mr. or MS Leader, can have all of the passion in the world for achieving a vision, however it does not mean anything if you don't show it! If you are afraid of what others may think about your passion, your over zealousness, your drive forward, then it will all be lost. Vision, is the number one key essential element, for without vision there is nothing to lead people to. Passion, however is the fuel that gets you there. If you keep that fuel hidden in the tank and don't use it, the engine is not going anywhere! Passion is the fuel that drives you to success and passion is the spark that ignites the fuel. Your passion must be displayed each and every day. Continually! You cannot tell your Vision to others, or worse yet, put it on a plaque on the wall, not say anything else about it and expect others to

"Don't ask yourself what the
world needs; ask yourself
what makes you come alive.
And then go and do that.
Because what the world needs
is people who have come
alive."

Harold Whitman

jump in and work their tails off to achieve it when they see you sitting back and not doing anything about it. YOU are the key element in success. NOTHING occurs in an organization that is not the responsibility or the accountability of the Leader. NOTHING! Everything that occurs, good AND bad starts and stops with you! The buck stops with you! As the saying goes, "You can delegate authority, but you cannot delegate responsibility!"

We must ultimately keep in mind that pursuing your Passion at all costs is foolhardy! You must let your passion propel you forward but at the same time, you must keep a sensible, logical head on your shoulders. As a leader you must maintain a balance between passion and reason. You must continually strive to achieve your passion but you must also keep it in check.

Every day, in every way, those you are leading need to see you out in front leading the way. This is no time to hide in your office, or say that you are too busy with other things, to be out talking to everyone, communicating your vision and its importance to the organization as well as your faith in the competence and ability of the people to make it happen. You are the cheerleader as well as the captain of the team. People throughout your organization need to see you and hear from you. This is not something you can delegate to those below you and hope they carry it forward. Like it or not, you are the one leading the charge. Teddy Roosevelt did not tell the Rough Riders to go conquer San Juan Hill, he led the charge up the hill to success!

"Nothing great in the world has ever been accomplished without passion."
Hebel

CHAPTER FIVE

EMPATHY

[2: *the action of understanding, being aware of, being sensitive to, and vicariously experiencing the feelings, thoughts, and experience of another of either the past or present without having the feelings, thoughts, and experience fully communicated in an objectively explicit manner*

A Leader without empathy
Runs the risk of being a tyrant!

Okay, I know that some of you reading this are asking yourselves, "Empathy, what does that have to do with leadership?" Empathy is not a word that has been mentioned often in management or leadership discussions until recently. In the not too distant past, leadership was generally thought of as being a part of management studies and not a separate field of its own. In the past, if someone was a manager, especially in the upper tiers of the organization, they were considered to be a leader. Today, however, a completely new and different view of leadership is emerging, requiring a better understanding of what leadership is and what is required of leaders. Also, a greater focus is on the abilities needed of leaders today. One of the greatest is the ability to have empathy. Today's workforce is vastly different than in the past and the average worker is looking for something different from their leaders. Workers today want to feel a connection with the work

173

If you could actually stand in someone else's shoes to hear what they hear, see what they see, and feel what they feel, you would honestly wonder what planet they live on, and be totally blown away by how different their "reality" is from yours. You'd also never, in a million years, be quick to judge again."
Unknown

they are doing, as well as the people in the organization.

Employees today do not want to be simply thought of as a "tool" or a "resource" for getting the job done. Most people working today have a growing need to feel as though they are a part of something greater than themselves and that what they are doing matters and has value. In other words, they are close to or at the top of Maslow's Hierarchy of Needs. The leader who can understand this and empathetically connect with those he or she is leading will experience greater success than ever before.

Not long ago, I had a conversation with a colleague, Toni McMurphy, a terrific Leadership development coach and consultant, who described a coaching session she had with one of her clients, Robert. It seems that this well educated, business-minded executive was having difficulty grasping the concept of 'empathy'. It seemed that the more they discussed the concept the more confused he became. He finally said, "I'm sorry but I just don't understand what you are talking about. How can one person feel what another person is feeling?" Toni thought for a moment and then told him that she was going to give him a homework assignment and she really wanted him to work hard on it over the weekend. She told him that she wanted him to really observe each member of his family and try to see the world through their eyes, to work to put himself in their shoes and feel what they were feeling.

When they next met, Robert was excited and said he had

"Some people think only intellect counts: knowing how to solve problems, knowing how to get by, knowing how to identify an advantage and seize it. But the functions of intellect are insufficient without courage, love, friendship, compassion and empathy."
Unknown

been really anxious to see her as he wanted to tell her about his experiences over the weekend. "When I first started," started Robert, "I tried to do what you asked by watching my wife, but for whatever reason, that just was not working. Later, when I was in the family room reading the paper, my eighteen-month old son, Jason came running into the room carrying his favorite stuffed animal, a ragged tiger he called Baba. No sooner had he entered the room than his older brother, Mike, who is three, came running into the room and snatched Baba from Jason's hands which instantly set Jason to wailing. Before I could say anything, Tommy, our oldest who is seven, came into the room and began wrestling with Mike. During the rough-housing Mike accidentally kicked Jason in the head and knocked him down. The more I watched what was going on in the room, the more I began to realize what Jason's world must be like. He is the smallest one in the family and I started to see how big everything must look to him. Here he was, totally powerless to what was going on around him. His older brothers could take what he had and there wasn't anything he could do about it and he was always at the mercy of others. After things calmed down and Jason was sitting in the middle of the floor playing with Baba, I really started to focus my attention on him and wondered what the world was like to him and I began to see how big everything must look to him. Immediately I felt a wave of total unconditional love for my son come over me. Jason, who was facing away from me, and all of a sudden he abruptly turned and looked me right in the eyes, jumped up, ran over to me, threw his arms around have been trying to teach me! I understood empathy and

"Two parts of empathy: Skill (tip of iceberg) and Attitude (mass of the iceberg)."

Unknown

really seeing things through the eyes of another and the my neck and gave me the biggest hug I had ever gotten from him." In that moment I finally understood what you power of having empathy.

Robert learned a great lesson about empathy due to Toni's wise guidance. But what does this mean in the workplace? Where does empathy play a role at work, and why is it a part of Leadership? Empathy is one of a Leader's greatest tools. To be able to totally focus on his/her followers and to understand where they are coming from and what they are going through, to totally understand their world as much as possible, gives the Leader greater insight in how best to lead. Also, it allows a connection to be made between the Leader and the followers. When followers sense that their leader is empathetic and understands their situation, a sense of trust develops because they sense that the Leader has their best interests at heart. Empathy, like active listening, which we'll talk about in Chapter 7, does not mean that you agree with the other's position or view of the world, it does mean however that you understand where they are coming from and how they see the world, and there is no greater gift to give someone than to understand things from their point of view and where they are in life.

Our ability to feel empathy towards someone, like so many things about who we are, is a function of our personality type. For some of us, feeling empathy towards someone and connecting with them on a deep level comes naturally, for others of us, we have to work

"We live in a culture that discourages empathy. A culture that too often tells us our principle goal in life is to be rich, thin, young, famous, safe, and entertained"
Barack Obama

at it. Empathy can be a very difficult thing to understand, and for those for whom it doesn't come naturally it can seem almost impossible and difficult to understand why it is so important. According to the Myers-Briggs Type Indicator, those who show a preference for Sensing (S), Thinking (T) and Judging (J) tend to live in a world of "what is" and the primary focus is no hard data, facts, figures, etc. whereas those who have a preference for Intuition (N), Feeling (F) and Perceiving (P) tend to live in the world of "what if." Feelings and intuition rule the day.

My personality type, according to Meyrs-Briggs is ENFP, which means that I have a preference for Extroversion, iNtuition, Feelings and Perception. Connecting with other people on a deep level, feeling and showing empathy and looking at what is possible has always been very easy for me. For those who focus on sensing, thinking and judging, these things tend to be a little more difficult, although they have the great ability to deal with the here and now and handle the routine and data very easily. For me, I find these things tedious and difficult. I once had a supervisor who told me, "Mike, I don't think I have ever worked with someone who has had so much difficulty dealing with details as you do. However, I am amazed at how easy it is for you to see the big picture and to look at what is possible and the things that we can do to make things better.

In terms of those who struggle with understanding empathy, it is not that they are uncaring, cold and unsympathetic; it is that other things take their focus

"The discoveries of how we can grow and the insights we need to have really come from the inside out. To have genuine empathy, not as a make-nice tool but as an understanding, is essential to the next step."

Patricia Sun

first! Our personality type is simply how we PREFER to function, it does not mean that we cannot adjust or adapt. In fact adjusting and adapting is exactly what we need to do in the business world, but we also need to realize the strengths that each other bring to the table based on their personality type.

Another aspect that can make it difficult to connect with someone through empathy is the "baggage" that we all carry. Now let's be honest and admit that "baggage" is something that we all have! We all carry baggage from our childhood that we took on from our parents, teachers, bullies at school and others in our life who we felt treated us unkindly. Some of us carry small pieces of baggage while others carry around a whole load of steamer trunks that at times are too large to carry. How we interact with each other is dictated in large part in how our "baggage" tells us to perceive each other. Someone with whom we work may be a really great co-worker and a terrific individual, but something about them stirs a memory deep within us and we might "see" someone from our past in their behavior and so we react to them with feelings of disdain, anger or deep sadness which causes us to respond to them in ways much differently than we would if we saw them for who they truly are. Looking beyond our baggage is difficult but extremely important. We'll discuss this more later when we talk about Knowledge and Emotional Intelligence.

By working on overcoming our "preferences" driven by our personality type, we can reach out to someone and connect with them empathetically and see things through

"The great gift of human beings is that we have the power of empathy, we can all sense a mysterious connection to each other."

Meryl Streep

their eyes before we rush to judging them based on our own personality type, or our own baggage.

Empathy is giving a part of yourself to the other person. At the deepest level, it is a heartfelt caring for another person and what goes on in their life. As a leader, empathy is about caring about the impact of your decisions on others in the organization, in the community and the world at large. Empathy is about understanding the needs and wants of those you are leading. It is about recognizing that you alone do not have all of the answers. It is about not leading from a vacuum. Empathy is about putting yourself in the shoes of those around you so you can better understand the impact of your decisions and what you are asking others to do.

We have already discussed the importance of Vision and how a leader must know where he or she is going in order to inspire others to follow. Empathy, gives the leader the sight needed to lead in the right direction. Empathy also gives the leader the real opportunity to connect with and inspire his or her followers. If a leader has a clear vision of where they want to go and they are able to truly connect with their followers, accomplishing the vision is almost a foregone conclusion.

Lack of Empathy creates Apathy

So what happens when there is a lack of empathy in leaders? Although it is not the sole instigator, it is a major contributor of apathy in an organization and apathy is the major cause of death in organizations large

"Self-absorption in all its forms kills empathy, let alone compassion. When we focus on ourselves, our world contracts as our problems and preoccupations loom large. But when we focus on others, our world expands. Our own problems drift to the periphery of the mind and so seem smaller, and we increase our capacity for connection - or compassionate action."
Daniel Golman

and small. Remember, Professor Robert Quinn says that entropy, or slow death is something that is a normal part of organizations and individuals and many people/organizations will choose entropy, or slow death, over deep change When those charged with getting the work done no longer care whether the work gets done, how it gets done or taking care of their customers, the organization is doomed to fail. Through a growing sense of apathy and not being a real part of what is happening workers all across the country have received the corporate lobotomy.

Many years ago I was selected to lead an all-employee involvement/problem solving effort for a seven-district, 3-State region of the company for which I worked at the time. We were making a huge effort in changing the management style from autocratic, top-down to a more open, employee centered way of doing things. Although a few of the managers with whom I worked were forward thinking and saw the value of what we were doing, or at least were aware enough to recognize that this was something the CEO wanted done, there were others who were not so adept at making the change. I likened a couple of these managers as having leadership skills a little to the right of Attila the Hun! If you were to look in the dictionary for the definition of 'autocratic' you would probably see their picture. To say that I found my job difficult and frustrating at times was an understatement. I was totally driven to bring about the changes we were implementing and often ran into a brick wall with managers who wanted nothing to do with it and often worked to circumvent what the teams were working on.

"People will forget what you said, people will forget what you did, but people will never forget how you made them feel."

Bonnie Jean Wasmund

On one particular occasion I returned to my office rather frustrated about something that had occurred in one of the districts and I stopped to talk to a colleague who was the manager of Occupational Safety and Health and several years my senior. As I stood in the doorway to his office, I began relating what had happened, venting my frustration and disappointment. Rich listened quietly for a few minutes and then said, "Mike come in, shut the door and sit down." After doing so, Rich asked, "Do you know what your problem is, my friend?" "No," I replied, "please tell me what my problem is." "Your problem," he continued, "is that you have not had the corporate lobotomy yet! Once you've had the corporate lobotomy you won't care so much and these things won't bother you anymore!" "Look around," he continued, "look at the people who come to work every day, do only what they are told to do and then go home at the end of the day without caring a great deal about what they do or what happens. They've all had the corporate lobotomy, and once you accept the fact that there is little anyone can do to change the system, then you won't really care a great deal either!" Bureaucracy is a determined beast that can destroy the enthusiasm of any worker. I told Rich that I would never accept the lobotomy and would leave the company before I let that happen. I've often thought about Rich's comment and have seen people in many different organizations who appear to have accepted the corporate lobotomy and that is terribly sad. Leaders who lead with a clear Vision, Integrity and Passion not only are more apt to arrive at the destination they have in mind, but they go a long way in eliminating the corporate lobotomy. I have seen first-hand the absolutely

"Empathy depends not only on one's ability to identify someone else's emotions but also on one's capacity to put oneself in the other person's place and to experience an appropriate emotional response"

Charles G. Morris

incredible, awe-inspiring power of people who are fully engaged and part of achieving a vision. There is nothing that cannot be achieved when people of a like-mind work together and have passion for what they are doing.

When a supervisor or manager truly acts with compassion and empathy, his or her employees will remember and respond in kind, often remembering that individual as one of the best leaders they had ever worked with. As I look back over the years, the people who stand out in my vast storehouse of memories were those who made a difference in my life by responding to me with empathy, understanding, and compassion and who recognized me for what I was able to contribute. For these people I worked harder and better than any others. I don't fondly remember, if at all, those who focused solely on getting more and more out of me simply to make their numbers look better.

How to Learn to be More Empathetic:

#1. Learn to listen! Listen with your eyes, head and your heart as well as your ears. Actively practice listening. It takes real effort to master but it must be done! Listen with your ears, your eyes, and your heart!

#2. Pay attention to what the other person is saying and look for whatever emotions they may be expressing.

#3. Spend time really focusing on what someone else is going through and put yourself in that situation while exploring your own feelings and emotions. Although we

"Could a greater miracle take place than for us to look through each other's eye for an instant?"

Henry David Thoreau

can never truly experience what someone else is experiencing, we can determine for ourselves how we might feel if we were to experience what they are experiencing.

#4. Be open to feedback from those around you. Those above you, your peers and most importantly, those who report directly to you

"Leadership is about empathy. It is about having the ability to relate to and connect with people for the purpose of inspiring and empowering their lives."

Oprah Winfrey

CHAPTER SIX
Knowledge

[2 *a* *(1):* the fact or condition of knowing something with familiarity gained through experience or association *(2):* acquaintance with or understanding of a science, art, or technique *b* *(1):* the fact or condition of being aware of something *(2):* the range of one's information or understanding <*answered to the best of my knowledge*> *c:* the circumstance or condition of apprehending truth or fact through reasoning]

A Leader without knowledge
is simply a follower of others!

Know your Baggage!

Knowledge is a powerful thing! The right knowledge in the possession of the right people can make great things happen. However, knowledge in the hands of people who use that knowledge simply for their own benefit, who hold onto knowledge as though it is their only source of power can create havoc and negativity in the workplace. To have true power, comes from having knowledge of oneself! Who are you? Who are you when no one else is around? Who are you when you are all alone with your thoughts? Knowing who you are, beyond others' perceptions of you, and even beyond your own perceptions of you, is immeasurable in its power to move you forward. Knowledge of oneself brings strength, focus, awareness and compassion for others. Over the course of the last few years I have asked many

*"I must follow my people, am
I not their leader?"*

Lao Tsu

people, this question: Who are you? Repeatedly, I ask this question in the leadership classes I facilitate. Without self knowledge, a leader runs the risk of being isolated and leading of a lack of awareness.

Naturally, when I ask someone that question they answer by telling me their name. "Is that all of who you are?" I ask. "Two words that form your name is the sum and total of who you are?" Often then, people will begin to stammer and search for the right words, but seldom find them. I recently facilitated a class on Leadership at Scott AFB, IL and I began by routinely asking that question. On the second day I asked who had been thinking about topics from the day before and, Linda, a woman who appeared to be in her mid-fifties said that she had thought about the question, "Who are you?" a great deal the evening before and was still asking herself that. She said, "In all my years, I have never really thought about it. I just assumed I knew, but now I am really questioning just how much of whom I believe I am I have taken on from others in my life." Very perceptive on Linda's part! How much of who you are have you taken on from the perceptions of others? I know in my life, I accepted a great deal of other peoples' perceptions until I really began looking internally and determining for myself who I am, and that process is a continuous process. Each day and every day! When we accept the perceptions of others, good, bad, or indifferent as being the "truth" of whom we are we run the risk of becoming lost. One thing I have learned over the years that has become a fundamental Truth, is that the perceptions of other people are really about them and not about me.

"Until we take how we see ourselves (and how we see others) into account, we will be unable to understand how others see and feel about themselves and their world. Unaware, we will project our intentions on their behavior and call ourselves objective."
Stephen Covey

When we have a perception of someone else, we are basing that perception on our own experiences, beliefs, history and none of those things are truly about the other person! I have come to learn that someone else's perception of me is really none of my business! Although it is nice to hear someone say good things about who we are, they are truly recognizing traits in us that they admire within themselves, which again, is about them. When we truly accept the awareness that what others say is about them and not us, and when we truly know the Truth of who we are, then we can listen to someone else's constructive criticism in a totally different way and accept it as something to look at but not take as a personal affront.

Who you are, is the result of many things. Your personality, your experiences, your education and your relationships have all played a part in developing your understanding who you are, however, for many of us, we often take the bumps and grinds of life with a very self-critical focus. We often mentally beat ourselves up saying things to ourselves when we do something wrong that we would never consider saying to our best friend in the same situation. Why is that? If we truly have a deep understanding of who we are, we learn the true value of the gifts we have, the talents we have and the abilities we have which can help us do great things. Unfortunately, many of us did not grow up in the perfect family and as a result we have baggage that we carry with us every day. We take it to work with us, to school, or any other place we go, and often we react to the current situation from the standpoint of that baggage and not from the Truth of

"If we value the pursuit of knowledge, we must be free to follow wherever that search may lead us. The free mind is not a barking dog, to be tethered on a ten foot chain."
Adlai E. Stevenson, Jr.

who we really are.

Baggage

This is a subject that frightens the daylights out of many people. I often have people tell me that my classes are different than any class they have ever attended. "This class is definitely not what I thought it was going to be!" is a routine statement. Most of the people follow this statement with something about how much they really enjoy the introspective approach I take and how much it really causes them to think about who they are and what they bring to the subject of leadership. Many take the discussion about baggage and how it impacts how they show up as a Leader seriously, however, unfortunately, for others, it is something that they do NOT want to talk about, let alone think about, and in some cases they become withdrawn and angry.

Where does our baggage come from? Well, basically it comes from our experiences in life. It comes from our family of origin, from experiences in school, our friends and others we encounter as we grow and learn. Many of us grew up in what is described as a dysfunctional family. Psychologyandspirit.com offers the following definition: "*A dysfunctional family is a family in which conflict, misbehaviour and even abuse on the part of individual members of the family occur continually, leading other members to accommodate such actions. ~ Children sometimes grow up in such families with the understanding that such an arrangement is normal. ~ Dysfunctional families are most often a result of the*

"Confront the dark parts of yourself, and work to banish them with illumination and forgiveness. Your willingness to wrestle with your demons will cause your angels to sing. Use the pain as fuel, as a reminder of your strength."
August Wilsonn

alcoholism, substance abuse, or other addictions of parents, parents' untreated mental illnesses/defects or personality disorders, or the parents emulating their own dysfunctional parents and dysfunctional family experiences."

Although a single-parent home is not inherently dysfunctional, what happens often is how the divorced parents treat each other in front of their children. They often take out unresolved animosity and anger on each other whether they are present or not, passing on negative feelings to their offspring. Also, the high level of substance abuse in America is at epidemic proportions and what happens often is that families will ignore it and pretend that it is not happening, all the while becoming co-dependent in their relationships with the abuser. Psychologists and psychiatrists estimate that over 90% of American families suffer from some sort of dysfunctionality. That seems like an overly large number, but if that is true, it certainly makes dysfunctional families the norm. So I suppose that having grown up in a severely dysfunctional family means I'm normal! Normal, maybe, in the statistical sense, but certainly not in terms of having a happy childhood.

Many years ago, I attended a self-help seminar to see if I could learn how to deal with the many "steamer trunks" of baggage I was carrying around and I ran into a woman who was wearing a very interesting tee-shirt. At the top of the front of the shirt was a stage and below the stage was row after row after row after row of chairs all the

"Know thyself? If I knew myself I'd run away!"
Johann Wolfgang Von Goethe

way down the front of the shirt. In the very middle of this vast sea of chairs sat one person. Above the stage there was a banner that read, "First Annual Convention of Children From Functional Families"

So what about you? Was there a sense of dysfunctionality in your family when you were growing up? If so, what baggage do you carry as a result? How is that baggage impacting "who you are?" And is that really "who you are?" Baggage is rather insidious. For many of us, we unfortunately let our baggage define who we are. I did this for a large portion of my life. My father, may he rest in peace, must have had a great deal of baggage he was dealing with. He had an issue with alcohol and when he drank, he was a very angry drunk and he would often take his anger out on me or my mother. He also would always looking for ways to, I believe, hide from his pain. I remember on different occasions where we would have visitors who happened to be taking a prescription pain killer for one reason or another and my father would ask if he could try some, and he always had a good excuse. We lived in a very rural area and there was a doctor in one nearby town who would write prescriptions for my father for whatever he wanted. This doctor was later sent to prison for wrongly writing prescriptions and peddling drugs, which of course made my father very angry! Through it all, I learned to be very fearful of my father and in a sense, men in general. Along with this fear, was the fear of authority. I was often afraid, or at least very uncomfortable, to talk to those I considered to be people of authority. Another, and maybe more important,

"Trust yourself, you know more than you think you do."
Benjamin Spock

message I got from my father, was that I wasn't "good enough." Mostly through his actions, I took on the

message that I was of little value. However, on several occasions, I remember him yelling at me, "Can't you ever do anything right?"

I say all of this, not to have a pity party for pity is the last thing we need to give someone. Pity does nothing but help the person remain a victim and unable to see the truth of who they are. I say this because these messages I accepted from my father greatly impacted my life and how I showed up in the world. Although I have been rather successful and received great feedback from others over the years, it all meant nothing! Why? Because inside I knew that I wasn't this "wonderful" person others saw in me. I was actually the person who wasn't good enough and who couldn't do anything right. Over the years, through the help of some very important people in my life, and a continuous focus on my part to question what I believed was true, I was able to see the Truth within myself and let my father's voice go away.

So, I ask again, who are you? What is the truth of who you are? Does how you show up in the world, how you see yourself as a leader, how you interact with others come from the Truth of who YOU are, or does it come from the perceptions others have had of you that you have accepted as your truth? Again, one of the greatest lessons I have learned in my life is that your opinion of me, or someone else's opinion of me is really none of my business!

"Any life, no matter how long and complex it may be, is made up of a single moment, the moment in which a man finds out, once and for all, who he is."

Unknown

I truly believe that leaders of the 21st century must be willing to look internally at who they are beyond perceptions they have taken on from others. Leaders of tomorrow have to be willing to do the work necessary to understand the Truth of who they are, how they show up in the world and what areas they truly need to work on to become a better leader and a better person. Of course, this is one reason I feel so strongly about Daniel Golman and his work on Emotional Intelligence (See Chapter 8).

Know your Personality

Another area that is very important for a 21st century leader to understand is their personality and how it impacts how they communicate with others, how they see the world, and in a sense, who they are. Another reason to really know and understand your personality is that it gives you a much better insight into those with whom you work and live. Many organizations today have sessions in which employees are asked to take a personality inventory in which a facilitator will discuss the impact personality has on others and what we do, and I think this is great. Where I believe many organizations fall short is in the mistaken belief that we can "hear it once and make immediate changes." That simply isn't true. Never has been and never will be. I don't care if it is a session on personality, company goals, communication or leadership. If we do not, organizationally, put processes in place to continually reinforce the concepts, ideas and high points in the sessions, then those things will be lost, if not at first, then over time. Remember, spaghetti-throwing training, or

"A man should instruct himself in the way he should go. Only then should he instruct others."

Buddha

communication, just does not work!

There are many great personality indicators and personality theories available, many of which are available online: Myers-Briggs Type Indicator, Social Styles Theory, DiSC, Ned Hermann's Whole Brain Theory. Each one looks at personality in a little bit different way and they all have something important to say. Although I personally prefer the MBTI, I believe that it is important for leaders to work through each one and understand what they each have to say, looking at what they have in common and where they differ. So how does personality impact the day-to-day operations? Here are some examples:

A few years ago I was hired by a company to set up a training department and a training records keeping system. I reported to the Director of HR and our offices were located on the 2nd floor of the building in the back corner. We didn't see a lot of traffic in our area as we were pretty much isolated which suited the Director's Staff Assistant very well. I didn't really pay a lot of attention until the HR department was moved down to the first floor across from the executive offices. Our area had two glass doors with an open area just inside. This is where the Staff Assistant sat. Because of this location, this entry area became Grand Central Station! This was the place where, it seemed, everyone stopped to talk. All of a sudden, the Staff Assistant became a very unhappy employee. She told me on different occasions that she absolutely hated to come to work since we moved our offices because she felt she could not get anything done.

"Ninety percent of the world's woe comes from people not knowing themselves, their abilities, their frailties, and even their real virtues. Most of us go almost all the way through life as complete strangers to ourselves."
Sydney J. Harris

When I asked her why she felt that way, she replied, "Because there are always people standing by my desk talking and it is so distracting!" I then realized that she was most likely someone who had a preference for introversion according to the MBTI. She preferred Introversion, she liked things quiet, she liked to be by herself, and she preferred to work by herself. Those who are "I's", typically find it very difficult to be the center of attention and find it distracting to work in a high-traffic, high-energy area. This is not always the case, but it can be a hindrance. This is just one example where if the HR Director had known this and could have made some very simple changes he could have had a much more efficient and productive, not to mention happier employee.

Another example: A couple of years ago, I was facilitating a class on Leadership for the Army Tank Command at Selfridge Air Guard Base in Warren, MI. In that class, I administered a "What's My Style" inventory, which gives the participants insight into how their personality impacts their behavior. In this particular inventory, the participants are asked to assign a total of five points between 18 pairs of adjectives on how much they feel each describes them. The points can be assigned 5-0, 4-1, 3-2, etc. Based on the participants responses they are then able to determine their "Style". After styles are determined, I would rearrange the class so that they were grouped by style. According to this inventory, the four styles are Direct, Systematic, Spirited, and Considerate. I always find it interesting to see how the sizes of the four groups end up. On this particular day, I had a fairly large group of Directs, those who like

"The greatest difficulty is that men do not think enough of themselves, do not consider what it is that they are sacrificing when they follow in a herd, or when they cater for their establishment"

Ralph Waldo Emerson

to work independently, take charge, get results, and are pragmatic and competitive. There was also a fairly even number of those who were Systematics, who typically like to make decisions based on facts, like details, are analytical, task-oriented, disciplined, calm and rational. Often, while administering this instrument, I would have someone ask if they could assign points in fractions, such as 1.5 or 3.5. Right away, I knew that this person was a Systematic because they typically like to be very precise.

I also had a group about the same size as the other two who were Considerates. Considerates are typically active listeners, like to work cohesively with others, value personal relationships, considers the feelings of others and are patient. This is the group I call the Kumbahya group, those who like to sit in a circle in a group hug, singing Kumbahya! The last of the four groups are those who are Spirited. Spiriteds generate excitement, are outgoing, tend to get caught up in dreams, are spontaneous, thrive on personal recognition and can be very persuasive. However, there was only one man sitting by himself at the Spirited table!

As I began to give the four groups the directions for the exercise I wanted them to work through within their group, a woman from the group of Considerates raised her hand. When I called on her, she asked, "Can I go sit with him?" pointing to the man sitting at the table by himself. I told her that for this exercise I needed her to stay with her selected group. I again began to give the instructions for the exercise and again someone from the Considerate group raised their hand. When I called on

215

"I do not pretend to know what many ignorant men are sure of."

Clarence Darrow

them, they asked, "Well, can he come sit with us?" "No" I replied, to which the man sitting alone said, "I'm fine by myself, I grew up an only child so being by myself does not bother me." "But you can't stay there by yourself!" several of those in the Considerate said in unison. This group of "people-oriented" individuals was so focused on their perceived needs of this one man sitting by himself that they literally were not going to let me continue until I said, "I am a Spirited as well, I will sit with him." That made everything okay for them, as long as he wasn't alone.

Understanding your personality gives you a wealth of knowledge about other people, who they are and why they do the things they do. It gives you as a leader, a chance to work with people on their terms and not on yours! I often hear people ask, "Why do I always have to adjust my style in working or communicating with other people? Why don't they have to adjust to my style?" I usually respond by saying, "Because you are the leader who wants to communicate better with other people and the leader who wants to be seen as wanting to make a difference." In a better world, we each would work to adjust our style when necessary. By doing this, we would both be working to improve the way we communicate and how we work together. Of course, understanding the impact of baggage on behavior, also adds a whole new dimension to the role of the leader.

Knowledge of self is vital. It comes from exploring and understanding our baggage and its impact on our behavior. Understanding our personality and its impact

"*Unless your heart, your soul, and your whole being are behind every decision you make, the words from your mouth will be empty, and each action will be meaningless. Truth and confidence are the roots of happiness.*"

Unknown

on our behavior and how we communicate and interact with others is vital to the role of a great leader.

However, there is much more about which to be knowledgeable. Tomorrow's leaders must know and understand generational differences. Today's workers are vastly different in many ways from their predecessors! They bring a totally different skill set, as well as totally different expectations. In one of my MBA classes I was talking about these differences and I mentioned an earlier segment on "60 Minutes" on CBS about the latest generation of workers to enter the workforce: http://www.cbsnews.com/video/watch/?id=4126233n&tag=mncol;lst;1. The segment was reported by Morley Safer and he said this new generation of workers were called Millenials, those born between 1980 and 1995. Safer stated during the report, "Millenials want to come to work by noon and still want to be CEO by Friday." Many companies, Safer reported, were spending a great deal of money hiring consultants to teach them how to deal with this new generation of workers. As I spoke to my class about this segment on 60 Minutes, one young lady raised her hand. When I called on her she said, "You're damn right we want to be CEO by Friday, and we deserve it! You owe us! Do you have any idea how much debt we are carrying when we graduate?" She continued, "Why should we have to wait for someone who has been on the job for years and is not interested in changing to finally decide to retire like they should and get out of our way?"

"The final mystery is oneself."
Oscar Wilde

The outlook of the Millennials is vastly different than that of those of the Baby Boomer generation, driven by what seems to be a totally different set of values. Where those of the Baby Boomer generation went to work for a company with the thought in mind of remaining until retirement, today's workers see nothing wrong with changing jobs several times in one year, while they find something they like to do at a company who likes them!

While some companies are quickly adapting, others are unfortunately lagging behind and are seemingly unwillingly to make the effort to look at the changing workforce and what is needed to meet the increasing demands of this new generation.

One of the companies recognized as being the best in working with the new, younger generation, as well as for its meteoric success, is Google. In a very short time, this company has totally changed how the environment within an organization is seen and its impact on workers. Many people of the older generations have had a difficult time understanding why any company would have a game room, encouraging its employees to take a break whenever they wanted and to go play games. Also, the latest trend seems to be nap rooms, where an employee can go take that much needed afternoon siesta! To those in the Baby Boomer generation the thought of playing games and taking naps at work is just about as foreign to their way of thinking as putting a man on the moon was to previous generations. In past generations there was no real focus on creativity, or thinking outside the box. Why? Because staying within the box and doing what

"I am afraid to show you who I really am, because if I show you who I really am, you might not like it--and that's all I got."

Sabrina Ward Harrison

the boss said was part of the hierarchical management system. There was very little, if any, leeway granted in how the work was to be accomplished. Today's workers are encouraged to be creative, to look at things differently and to come up with new solutions to age old problems.

As a member of the Baby Boomer generation, I can say that when I entered the job market, there was very little thought given to having a career unless you were a member of the upper to upper-middle class where it was a given that college was a certainty. Having grown up in a very poor, rural area, thought of college was, in many cases, a dream. Although I fully intended to go to college, at the time I had no idea of a particular career, it was all about what would give me the best job. Finding a good company to work for, one with which you could spend your entire working life, was the primary focus. Today's generation is not interested in this approach. In their minds, they see this as settling and they saw their parents work for 20 or 30 years for a company and then get laid off with little or no retirement benefits. The Millenials of today see their 20's as a time to really find out what they specifically like to do and then work at achieving in that area, rather than just working for a company that pays well. Where they work is not as important as what they like to do!

Recently, I was asked to speak at a two-day all-hands meeting of a Federal agency about tomorrow's leaders, change and culture. Part of the reason they wanted to focus on these topics was because they had recently

"Actions have consequences....first rule of life. And the second is this: You are the only one responsible for your own actions."

Holly Lisle

changed Directors but part was because they saw that many of their upper management people would soon be retiring and they wanted to focus on a new leadership style. In preparing what I was going to say, I spoke to a couple of people in the organization and found that the previous Director had been rather autocratic in his approach, made all of the decisions and ruled with somewhat of an iron first. The new director told me that her approach was one that was totally opposite. In fact, during the meeting, she spoke at length about how she did not have all of the answers and she was looking to everyone in the room to work with her so they could come up with the best answers together. She repeatedly emphasized the same things I stressed during my time, and that is an abundance of knowledge and untapped potential in the workers of today! A leader's true job is to do whatever is necessary to bring that vast untapped potential and the total capacity available to the forefront and allow everyone to be a part in reaching the vision of the organization.

Life-long Learning

Acquiring knowledge should be a never ending quest. It should constantly be in the forefront of the leader's mind and a constant focus. Whenever we become complacent, or begin to think that we have the answers, or believe that we "do not have time" the game is over. At that point a leader ceases to lead and begins to dictate, following his/her own agenda. Remember, it is not YOUR agenda, but the agenda of the organization, and the organization consists of the hearts, minds, intent and

"Truth is rarely pure and never simple."

Oscar Wilde

willingness of each and every person who is a part of the organization. Focusing on the importance of being a life-long learner is important to foster throughout the organization. Organizations that succeed in the future are going to be those that offer their employees learning and self-development opportunities while continually focusing on how things can be better, how the organizational can be better. To succeed, the past needs.
to be looked at as a place to learn about what worked and what didn't work and how that information can be used to move forward The greatest piece of knowledge that a leader can possess, is that leadership is not about himself or herself. The paradox of leadership is that a true leader is both the most important person in the organization and the least important at the same time. Leadership is a true dichotomy by nature and once we begin to think that it is all about us, not only the battle, but the war itself, is lost. True leadership is about having a very clear understanding of followers. Knowing who your followers are, what they need and what they want, and building relationships with your followers. In years past, building relationships with individual workers was discouraged because it was believed that managers were supposed to remain impartial, especially in times of administering punishment. True leaders believe that punishment of any kind is an absolute last resort. Long before getting to punishment there should be a focus on assisting the individual employee to discover on their own the areas in which they need to improve, discovering the things that are holding themselves back and how to move beyond these roadblocks. This is done by the leader being a caring, empathetic coach, helping

"In matters of truth and justice, there is no difference between large and small problems, for issues concerning the treatment of people are all the same."

Albert Einstein

the employee discover a greater truth for themselves.

The focus has to be on each individual employee, treating them as an individual, recognizing their individual needs, wants, talents and abilities and working together to see how they can best be placed in the organization to maximize not only the benefit to the organization, but to the individual worker herself.

What is True!

The final thing I would like to offer that a leader must have is the ability to continually strive to discover what is True. What are the things that you know to be true? What are the things that you absolutely know without a shadow of a doubt are true at all times? Are you really sure they are true? The interesting thing that I have discovered is that many of the things that I was taught growing up to be "True" simply were others' perceptions of what was true and were not actually true for me. I believe that in order to have a good knowledge of who we are, we need to question the things that we were taught to be true. What things in your life that you have learned "to be true" that you have accepted without really questioning whether or not it fits for you? Also, how have those things impacted your life and how are they continuing to impact your life. How have those "truths" impacted the way you have interacted with others. When someone offers a different 'truth' than what you believe to be true, how do you react? Are you willing to truly listen, explore the possibility, and question your own beliefs and why you believe what you believe to be true?

"Zeal without knowledge is fire without light."

Thomas Fuller

Or do you steadfastly believe what you have always thought to be true without question, without dialogue and shut the other person off because what they are saying does not fit your "Truth?"

I talked about the "truths" that we are taught without much thought as to whether they fit for us or not in one of the classes I was facilitating and I told the story about how I grew up in a very small town in one of the poorest counties in Missouri. In a room where participants were almost evenly mixed between Whites and Blacks, I said that in the town where I grew up, there was no one who did not look like me. In fact, there was no one in the county who did not look like me, and the unspoken "truth" was that the sun had better not set on someone who did not look like me. As soon as I said that, one young African-American man said, "We all know what that is. It's a sun-down town." I agreed and related that while growing up, I heard all of the racial slurs, jokes, negative comments imaginable about people of color, so that when I left home at the age of seventeen, I had a definite 'truth' about people of color and who they were and what they were capable of, which wasn't much. Fortunately, one of the first people I worked with on the evening shift was a young Black man, and Clyde taught me a lot about my wrong thinking and through him, I began to see a new, and much better, truth! I am so grateful for the opportunity to learn that very important fact that I have continually worked to learn the other 'truths' that I learned and have held on to that are not necessarily true. It is imperative for leaders to fully search for their own "truths" within themselves and to

"I try to learn from the past, but I plan for the future by focusing exclusively on the present. That's where the fun is."

Donald Trump

search out those things they erroneously believe, especially when it comes to dealing with those he or she is leading. Often in an organization a certain truth will be developed about the potential of this employee or that employee and is this really a truth? Or is it someone's perception that was spread from one person to another until it became a "truth" that maybe even the employee himself bought into?

When it comes to leadership and knowledge, there are many different things a leader needs to know. The exciting part of the quest is that the journey of learning never ends. It is incumbent on leaders of tomorrow to instill the quest for knowledge within the very heart of the organization. Peter Senge, stated in *The Fifth Discipline* that organizations must become "learning organizations" constantly focusing on how we can be better, do better, and live better, beyond just achieving a better profit margin. If we focus simply on the bottom line we may be successful, but not nearly so if we engage the hearts, minds and souls of everyone in the organization! There is an unbelievably vast storehouse of knowledge, talent, ability and willingness that is mainly going untapped in many organizations and it is the responsibility of tomorrow's leader to recognize and tap into this vast storehouse and unleash the potential of the employees she is leading!

"The time is always right to do what is right."

Martin Luther King, Jr.

CHAPTER SEVEN

Communication

> **3 a:** *a process by which information is exchanged between individuals through a common system of symbols, signs, or behavior <the function of pheromones in insect communication> ; also : exchange of information* **b:** *personal rapport*

A Leader who cannot communicate a clear vision is doomed to fail!

"A process by which information is exchanged between individuals," sounds easy doesn't it? We are born into a world in which communication is essential. Immediately after birth, as babies we begin communicating that we are cold, hungry, etc. and as we grow older, we learn to articulate words and attach meaning to the words, (or symbols) we speak. Communicating is the easiest thing in the world, right? Well, maybe we should say that talking is the easiest thing in the world, but communicating, well that's a different story. Why? Why does it become so much more difficult to communicate the meaning of our messages as we grow older? We all speak the same language, don't we? Or do we? When we are speaking English to another person whose first language is English, communication still does not occur, more often than not, why?

A simple example: Jerry is eighteen years old and just graduated from high-school with dreams of going to

"People say conversation is a lost art; how often I have wished it were."

Edward R. Murrow

college and becoming an Aeronautical Engineer. He is a rather bright young man, having made mostly straight A's in high school and graduating in the top 5% of his class. Everyone tells him he has a bright future ahead and he is anxious to get started. For the last two years he has worked at the local fast-food restaurant, and he has been longing for a "real" job. Just last week, Jerry was hired as a mail clerk in a local very prestigious engineering firm and he is extremely motivated to do the best possible job he can, with hopes that it would turn into steady summer employment while he goes to college. Shortly after arriving at work this morning, Jerry is walking through the executive offices when the CEO, James Landers, spots him and says he has something important he wants him to do for him and asks him to come into his office. Jerry has met Jim already and is really impressed that Jim has something important he wants him to do. "Now's my chance to really shine," David thought as he walked into Jim's office. He really wanted to do a great job so Jim would know he was a good worker and very capable. As Jerry walked into Jim's office, Jim picked up a sheet of paper off of his desk and told Jerry, "This is extremely important and I need you to do it ASAP as I have a meeting to get to. I want you to take this letter into the storeroom and burn it. Can you do that for me?" "Sure!" Jerry responded enthusiastically, wondering why Jim would want this important looking letter burned, but determined he was going to do the best possible job, "I'll do it right away!" "Come back as soon as you're done," responded Jim.

Jerry left Jim's office and headed to the storeroom, stop-

"The dead might as well try to speak to the living as the old to the young."
Willa Cather

ping by the break room where he had seen some matches earlier. When he entered the storeroom, he found a metal trashcan and immediately set the letter on fire. After it had completely burned, he returned to Jim's office and reported that he had burned the letter.

Jim replied, "That's great, Jerry, I appreciate it, where is it, I'm late for my meeting?" Jerry was a bit confused, "It's, uh, it's in the storeroom," Jerry stammered. "What do you mean, it's in the storeroom?" Jim asked, "I told you I'm in a hurry, why did you leave it in the storeroom?" Jerry felt the blood rush to his face and he was getting really worried that something was wrong, "Well, I burned it like you asked me too, and I threw the ashes in the trash," Jerry responded. "ASHES!" Jim yelled, "What do you mean ashes?" I wanted you to make a copy, you idiot!" "I cannot believe that you would be stupid enough to actually burn that letter, it was extremely important and the only copy!" "You're fired!" Jim roared.

Although you may be a bit incredulous that the above story could actually take place, it was once reported in a textbook on communication as being a real-life situation. Another all too similar scenario occurred when a young man was hired by a manufacturing company to work the 2nd shift. The company had a lot of water storage tanks out in the yard and the young man was told by his supervisor, "It's going to be pretty cold tonight, so before you go home, I want you to go out in the yard and crack the valve on each of those tanks." When the day shift arrived the next day, they found that someone had taken

"Two monologues do not make a dialogue."
Jeff Daly

a hammer and broken the valve on each of the tanks in the yard. Instead of opening each of the valves a little bit, the young man had understood his boss to mean something different. We might argue that each of these young men was far from brilliant for doing what they did, however, in their minds they did exactly as they were asked to do. In each situation communication did not occur! Just because we tell someone something that is crystal clear to us, does not mean that it is equally clear to the other person. Now, in each of these scenarios, what if the supervisor had asked, "Now do you understand what I want you to do?" What would each of the young men replied? Certainly, it would have been, "Yes, I do." They understood exactly what they interpreted the boss said. If the supervisors had asked, "Tell me what it is I want you to do," in most cases, I believe the young men would have most likely responded with, "You want me to take this letter into the storeroom and burn it," or "You want me to crack the valve on each of the tanks in the yard," in which case they would have signaled that clear communication had occurred, right? NO! Repeating back the words we hear does not signify that communication has occurred. If we look back at the definition of communication at the beginning of the chapter, we find that it says that communication is "a process by which information is exchanged between individuals through a common system of symbols..." The problem in both of these situations is that both parties in each scenario had a different 'system of symbols.' The words, or symbols used did not have common meanings.

"Developing excellent communication skills is absolutely essential to effective leadership. The leader must be able to share knowledge and ideas to transmit a sense of urgency and enthusiasm to others. If a leader can't get a message across clearly and motivate others to act on it, then having a message doesn't even matter."

Gilbert Amelio
President and CEO
National SemiConductor Corp.

I once read that in business, approximately $1 Billion is lost every day due to miscommunication. That's Billion with a B! That is a lot of money lost, simply because we do not know how to effectively communicate! Now you may argue that figure is incorrect, but I also would guess that you can come up with many situations of your own where miscommunication caused you, your organization, or someone else you know to lose a good deal of money due to a misunderstanding.

Why is communication so difficult?

If we look at what goes on in the process of communication we begin to get an understanding of what is going on. In a typical communication model, we have a sender and a receiver, a message, a medium and a process called encoding and decoding. The sender of the

message must encode the message, which means that the words must be formulated in such a way as to say what the sender means to say. The receiver of the message must then decode that message in order to understand the meaning of the message just received. It seems all

"The void created by the failure to communicate is soon filled with poison, drivel and misrepresentation."
C. Northcote Parkinson

straight forward enough that there shouldn't be any real problems, right? Well, it is the encoding and decoding of the message where we get into serious trouble. If we look at what goes into the encoding process, we find that many things impact the words or symbols we choose to say, how we say those words or symbols and the medium in which we deliver the message. A small number of the factors that might impact how we encode a message might include:

Gender	Age
Baggage	Experience
Education	Biases
Judgments	Family of Origin
Ethnicity	Region of Origin
Emotional Intelligence	IQ
Values	Status

And, of course, these same factors impact the decoding of the message by the receiver. When we look at the process of communicating in this manner, is there any wonder why we have so much trouble communicating? Naturally, no two people are alike; no two people have had the same experiences, backgrounds and perceptions. Also, we should keep in mind that there is a primary factor that impacts heavily on both sender and receiver: personality!

Much has been written about personality, how it is developed, where it comes from, how it impacts how we communicate, etc. that I don't believe we need to go into great detail here. However, if you are interested in

"I know you believe you understand what you think I said, but I'm not sure you realize that what you heard is not what I meant."

Robert McCloskey

reading more about how you communicate due to your personality type and how to improve your communication with others in your life at home and at work, I highly recommend, *"Please Understand Me"* by John Kiersey and Marilyn Bates. Kiersey and Bates began studying temperament and its impact on communication and found that their work fell in very close alignment with the Meyrs-Briggs Type Indicator. They offer a version of the MBTI at the back of their book and it is a very effective way to determine your personality type as well as others in your life. The authors go to great lengths detailing how each personality and each temperament prefers to communicate and how, if we learn to adjust our own communication patterns to meet the personality and temperament of the person to whom we are speaking, we will go great distances in communicating in a more comprehensive manner.

I often speak at great lengths about the impact of communication in teams and how personalities come into play. As someone who has always been fascinated by personality and the judgments we make about others in our lives based solely on the personality traits they were born with, I find Kiersey's and Bates' work to be a great source of information. Over the years, I have received a great deal of training in team formation, team leadership and facilitation and find that many organizations are sadly lacking when it comes to understanding the true functioning of teams and what is needed to help teams become stellar performers. One way to really help teams become better in the way they operate is to provide

"Think like a wise man, but communicate in the language of the people."
William Butler Yeats

ongoing training on team dynamics and communication. For example: The Meyrs-Briggs Type Indicator (MBTI) is based on the work of Carl Jung, Austrian psychiatrist and protégé of Sigmund Freud. Jung studied personalities and found similar traits in different individuals that he categorized into four different dyads: Extroversion/Introversion; Sensing/Intuition; Thinking/Feeling and Judging/Perceiving. Jung believed that those who have a preference for extroversion get their energy from the outside world, whereas those who prefer introversion get their energy from within themselves. Those who are E's tend to talk openly and freely, often speaking before really thinking things through, so in a team, or group meeting, they may throw out ideas that at first blush may seem somewhat silly or even ridiculous. Often, those who have a preference for extroversion will themselves be the first to counter what they've said once they hear it spoken out loud. I's on the other hand generally are very thoughtful and often hesitate to say anything until they have things well thought out in advance, making sure every 'i' is dotted and 't' is crossed. I's want to make sure that they fully understand what they are going to say before the say it, often to the point of not saying anything at all. If teams do not know and understand this simple bit of information, their communication patterns may be adversely affected. 'I's,' when they hear an 'E' saying a lot of things that are not well thought out, they may judge that person as being shallow, a big-mouth, or not contributing much value to the team. On the other hand, when an 'E' doesn't hear much from an 'I' he or she may think that that person is not a team player, unmotivated, not with the program, or

"The problem with communication ... is the illusion that it has been accomplished."

George Bernard Shaw

just simply doesn't care about what the team is working on. These judgments can and do often lead to communication problems because they impact the way we judge the other person and limit, and at times, the contact we want to have with them. Understanding the various aspects of your personality, as well as the personalities of others not only gives you the opportunity to better understand how to communicate better, it also give you a better awareness of the behaviors of other people and to understand that the things for which you might judge them harshly may indeed be strengths to be used. Those who are "E's" are great at coming up with ideas which can then be taken by those who are "I's" and processed more fully, and together they each have something of tremendous value to offer. When we fully understand personality traits and look at the positive aspects and how different personalities can be used on a team to achieve better success, everyone wins!

So how do we know what type or personality style another person is? The more we learn about our own personality, the more we learn about other people and if we really learn type and personality styles we can often determine the style of other people when we get to know them. When we get to know someone, we learn whether they like to regenerate their energy by being alone, or if they really enjoy being a part of a large, high energy group. We also learn whether they like to deal with details or if they are have the ability to focus on the big picture, and so on. The first time I worked through the MBTI, I learned a great deal about myself, including some of the things that I often considered to be negative

"Communication is the real work of leadership."
Nitin Nohria

traits or behaviors that were actually traits of my personality type which I brought with me when I entered this world and were in fact positive traits! I did learn a great deal about myself, but I also learned a great deal about my wife, and why she would drive me crazy at times! Part of my job duties included serving as a Community Relations Representative. I was actively involved in many civic and social organizations, and often had evening meetings, some of which were dinner meetings, and occasionally my wife would be invited to attend. It got to where I could mark it on the calendar, two to three days before the event, the questions would start, "How many people are going to be there?" "What's the agenda going to be?" "Where is everyone going to sit?" "What is the menu going to be?" "What are they going to do after dinner?" and of course, the best one, "What is everyone going to wear?" As the questions continued, I would find myself getting more and more exasperated, not because I did not have the answers to any of the questions, but because I did not see how these questions were of any importance, I found these questions to be somewhat tiresome.

What I learned in the session in which I worked through the MBTI, is that the need for detail about what was going to happen was a function of her personality type. Data and detail to my wife helped her feel in control of her world because it gave her a better sense of what was going to happen. Again, when team members know these aspects about each other, it can improve communication and understanding. My type is one in which I do not focus a great deal of effort on knowing

"The more elaborate our means of communication, the less we communicate."

Joseph Priestly

'what is,' rather I tend to focus more on 'what might be.' The real magic occurs in a team environment when every member knows and understands the real capacity of what they each have to offer and to accept each other as a fully contributing member. In so many organizations, the word "team" has become a nonsensical term that is bandied about endlessly. Calling a department or a group of employees a team does not make them a team!!! To truly have a team, regardless of size or level, within an organization takes a focus not only on task behaviors, those behaviors required to accomplish a task or achieve a vision, but it takes maintenance behaviors. Maintenance behaviors are focused to increase the team's knowledge, awareness, understanding and focus of who they are as a team, who everyone on the team is and what skills, attributes, talents and abilities each person brings to the team. Understanding personality and how to effectively use personality differences to enhance team effectiveness are wonderful, and mandatory, team maintenance tools that can help the team achieve great success.

Listening

There is no part of communication that is more misunderstood or underutilized than the skill of listening! Whenever I talk about communication in my classes, I ask "Who in this room is a good listener?" Often, several hands would go up. I would then ask, "What do you do that makes you a good listener?" The answers I have received were across the board. Occasionally I would get some very good responses, indicating that

*"Two men in a burning house
must not stop to argue"*
African Proverb

maybe this person was very good at listening. However, I would often get some rather interesting answers that bordered on disbelief! One day, when I asked this question, a young lade raised her hand and said that she was an excellent listener. When I asked her what she did that made her a good listener, she responded by saying, "Well, I work in a cubical and I often have someone come into my cube to talk to me about a particular project of something else going on in the office, and I can listen very well while I continue to work on reading and responding to my email." If there is a part of you right now that is thinking that she was correct in saying that she was a good listener, I hate to burst your bubble, but working on emails, or anything else for that matter, does not make you a good listener!

Listening involves focusing 100 percent of our attention on the speaker, without distractions, without judgments, and without thinking about how we are going to respond when, and if, they ever stop talking! Listening is extremely difficult to do because we have to set our ego aside and listen with our heart as wells as our ears. We also have to listen with our eyes, looking for non-verbals that connect or disconnect with the words being said. Listening means putting all other things aside, stopping what you are doing, giving the speaker the gift of your full attention.

"When someone really hears you without passing judgment on you, without taking responsibility for you, without trying to mold you, it feels damn good. When I have been listened to, when I have been heard, I am able to re-perceive my world in a new way and go on. It is astonishing how elements that seem insoluble become soluble when someone listens. How confusions that seem irremediable become relatively clear flowing streams when one is heard."

Carl Rogers

To really be a good listener:

1. Stop what you are doing and meet the person on their level. Both should either be standing or sitting!
2. Turn off any distracting noise if possible, radios, ipods, etc.
3. Clear your mind of your own personal thoughts.
4. Make eye contact but do not stare.
5. Nod your head or offer phrases such as "Go on," "I see" or some other phrase to let them know that you are paying attention.
6. Do not be thinking about what you have to do later, what you are going to have for lunch or dinner, errands you have to run, or other thoughts that are totally disjointed from the current conversation.
7. Do NOT interrupt!!!
8. When there is a pause in what the speaker is saying, repeat what you heard the speaker say, but do not repeat the words. Start out by saying, "Before you go on, I want to make sure that I am understand what you have said. I understood you to say...... repeating what you understood in your own words.
9. If there is something you do not understand, ask for clarification.
10. Often times, someone just wants to be heard. Do not try to problem solve unless you are asked to do so!

"If there is any one secret of success, it lies in the ability to get the other person's point of view and see things from his angle as well as your own."
Henry Ford

11. Do not give advice! Use questions to help the other person discover what they need!

Good listening skills take time, effort and dedication to acquire. Because you may not have used these skills in the past, when you begin to work on sharpening your listening skills, others may ask, "What are you doing?" and may be very surprised and impressed that you care enough to really listen to them. Since actively listening to someone is the most sincere and special gift you can give someone, you might respond by saying, "You are important to me and what you have to say is important to me. I am working on improving my listening skills so that I can better understand where you are coming from and what I can learn from your point of view."

Today's leaders, in order to secure a successful future, need to lead in a way that gets everyone in the organization onboard and working together. The best way to accomplish this is to learn to communicate effectively and listen continually. Without either ability, the leader is lost and doomed to fail!

"Listening is a magnetic and strange thing, a creative force. The friends who listen to us are the ones we move toward. When we are listened to, it creates us, makes us unfold and expand."

Unknown

CHAPTER EIGHT

Emotional Intelligence

[1 : of or relating to emotion*; 1 a (1): the ability to learn or understand or to deal with new or trying situations :* reason *; also : the skilled use of reason (2): the ability to apply knowledge to manipulate one's environment or to think abstractly as measured by objective criteria (as tests)]*

A Leader without emotional intelligence
is at the mercy of circumstances!

For the majority of my life, I was not emotionally intelligent! Instead of acting and responding appropriately to life, I reacted to it, often with negative consequences. I was at the mercy of life's circumstances, and primarily I was at the mercy of the whims of other people. I was continually reacting in defense of imagined and perceived slights, put-downs and negative comments from others. It often did not matter what was said, I would often take it as a put-down or a slight of my abilities or even worse about me as a person. I never felt as though I measured up, was good enough, or could "play with the big-boys." There were often times when I would receive compliments but those kind words had little if any impact on me. Why? Because I didn't believe those words could actually be about me. I didn't believe in myself. I spent a great deal of time reacting from the baggage in my life. I was continually listening to my father's voice telling me I

"It is very important to understand that emotional intelligence is not the opposite of intelligence, it is not the triumph of heart over head -- it is the unique intersection of both."

David Caruso

couldn't do anything right! I let my actions be determined by the way I saw things through my baggage. I wrote at some length about baggage earlier but I want to re-emphasize the impact that baggage had on me, my career and how I showed up in the world. I remember one particular instance in which I was working as a Lead Facilitator for a quality improvement/employee involvement effort, working with a group of managers who, outside of a small number, were resistant to change, reluctant to do what was needed in order to make the change requested by the CEO of the company, and in some cases downright belligerent! On one particular day during a staff meeting with the vice-president to whom we all reported, a manager from another department, who was on the agenda, said to me after I spoke about some of the changes we needed to make, "Mike, I thought the word facilitator meant to make things easier." I immediately reacted in a very negative, passive-aggressive manner by glaring at him and becoming very sullen and withdrawn, taking his words as a personal affront. I have often looked back on that moment and realized that I had taken his comment entirely erroneously. He was attempting to be humorous, given the situation; however I took it as a personal slur, that I was the problem and I resented it. I reacted from my baggage. As he was older than me, I saw my father when I looked at him and I reacted according to my baggage.   Sometime later, my boss, during a performance review, told me that he believed that I needed to get better control of my emotions because I reacted out of anger too often. Again, I took his comment as a personal affront, however he was 100%

"Emotional Intelligence is a way of recognizing, understanding, and choosing how we think, feel, and act. It shapes our interactions with others and our understanding of ourselves. It defines how and what we learn; it allows us to set priorities; it determines the majority of our daily actions. Research suggests it is responsible for as much as 80% of the "success" in our lives."

Friedman, et al

accurate. Because of my baggage, I carried around a great deal of deep seated anger and was ready to unleash it in a heartbeat. As a result, my rise within the company was limited and I knew that I would not go further until I got control of my baggage and learned the Truth of who I was! The one thing I by working through my issues is that we either learn to deal with the baggage, or the baggage deals with us!

Daniel Goleman

In real estate, the three first three rules are 1) location, 2) location and 3) location, when it comes to Emotional Intelligence the first three rules are: 1) Daniel Goleman, 2)Daniel Goleman, and 3) Daniel Goleman. Goleman, more than any other person has brought the importance of emotional intelligence into the business environment.

Goleman was a scientific writer who ran across the term 'emotional intelligence' in an article published in a small academic journal by two psychologists, John Mayer and Peter Salovey. Goleman became intrigued with the concept of emotional intelligence and how it might contribute to success in the business world. Goleman explains that at the time of his discovery of the article by Mayer and Salovey, mental intelligence or IQ was the preeminent predictor of success. Businesses, for years, had used IQ tests as a hiring tool, as well as a predictor of success. Nothing could have been further from the truth. In my own case, I had been blessed with a fair amount of mental intelligence, however my emotional intelligence, or lack thereof, was the true predictor of my success.

"In the last decade or so, science has discovered a tremendous amount about the role emotions play in our lives. Researchers have found that even more than IQ, your emotional awareness and abilities to handle feelings will determine your success and happiness in all walks of life, including family relationships."

John Gottman

I'm certain that almost everyone has encountered the supervisor, manager or other person in charge, (I will not call them a leader!) who has seemingly lost control of his or her emotions and has gone off the deep end screaming and yelling due to some transgression (or perceived transgression) of an employee. These tirades may, in some way, make the person doing the yelling feel better, but they do no good whatsoever for the employee and certainly not for the organization. What it does, is create an atmosphere of fear and tension in which few people want to work. Always waiting for another outburst from the boss, employees spend more time watching their backs or looking for another job than they do being productive and working to find new and better ways to accomplish what needs to be done. These tyrant managers, I believe, are reacting to situations in their lives from the standpoint of their baggage. Many times in the past, organizations would promote individuals based on seniority and competence in the current position, giving little thought to the things needed by the next higher position.

Just because someone was really good as a machinist, or a scientist in a lab, does not always mean that they will be good leading people. It simply means that they were knowledgeable and capable of performing in a specific role. Today's leaders, and certainly leaders of tomorrow need a very specific skill set if they are going to succeed and the organization is going to succeed. That skill set is primarily about who they are when no one is looking, it is about how they interact with others, it is about their self image and whether they are capable of seeing where

"If your emotional abilities aren't in hand, if you don't have self-awareness, if you are not able to manage your distressing emotions, if you can't have empathy and have effective relationships, then no matter how smart you are, you are not going to get very far."

Daniel Golman

they can go, as well as their ability to influence others!

In an article he wrote for the Harvard Business Review, *"What Makes a Leader?"* Goleman cites the findings of the late David McClelland. McClelland, long a recognized leader in the field of human and organizational behavior, found in a 1996 study of a global food and beverage company that *"when senior managers had a critical mass of emotional intelligence capabilities, their divisions outperformed yearly earnings goals by 20%. Meanwhile, division leaders without that critical mass underper-formed by almost the same amount."* This study, I would say pretty much says it all as to the importance of emotional intelligence capabilities in the success of leaders!

Self-Awareness

The first component of emotional intelligence means having a deep understanding of your

The Five Components of
Emotional Intelligence at Work

	Definition	Hallmarks
Self-Awareness	The ability to recognize and understand your moods, emotions and drives, as well as their effect on others	Self-confidence; realistic self-aware-ness; self-deprecating sense of humor

"Good leaders develop through a never-ending process of self-study, education training, and experience."
Manual on Military Leadership

Self-Regulation	The ability to control or redirect impulses and moods; the propensity to suspend judgment – to think before acting.	Trust-worthiness and integrity; com-fort with ambiguity; openness to change
Motivation	A passion to work for reasons that go beyond money or status; a propensity to pursue goals with energy and persistence.	Strong drive to achieve; optimism, even in the face of failure; organiza-tional commitment
Empathy	The ability to understand the emotional makeup of other people; skill in treating people according to their emotional re-actions.	
Social Skill	Proficiency in managing relationships and build-ing networks; an ability to find common ground and build rapport.	Effectiveness in leading change; per-suasiveness; ex-pertise in building and leading teams.

Harvard Business Review

emotions, strengths weaknesses, needs and drives. So I will ask you the question I repeatedly ask in the leadership classes I facilitate. Who are you? No, I am not looking for your name, or your job title, or your relationships. Who are you? Do you know? I mean do you REALLY know who you are? I don't know about you, but for many, many years I didn't even want to think about that question. I didn't want to really look into the depths of who I am for fear of what I might see. Because of the way I was raised, I had a very deep and abiding fear that if I really looked inside, I might find out that my father was right, and that I really couldn't ever do anything right, or that I was of very little value.

"To live is to choose. But to choose well, you must know who you are and what you stand for, where you want to go and why you want to get there."

Kofi Annan

Although you may not have these particular feelings, are there other feelings that come from your baggage that may resonate with you? I would be willing to bet that you have your own fears and your own way of reacting at times that run counter to how you would like to react. Why do I say this? How do I know? Because I am a student of human nature. I love to learn about personalities and why we do what we do. I also know that virtually all of us spend a great deal of our energy dragging around our 'baggage' from the past. Oh, for the most part, we do a pretty good job of keeping it under control. We struggle and internally argue with ourselves and with the "voices" of the past, and do everything we can to keep the dragons in their lair. God forbid that one of those dragons should ever slip out of the cave when someone else was around! And even worse, it is too frightening to ever think about entering the dragon's lair and slay the lot of them. However, that is exactly what we need to do. In order to grow emotionally, and become the true person we are, beyond all of the nonsense our baggage tells us, is at the heart of becoming a leader. Becoming more self-aware is truly an exciting journey. Some people are fairly comfortable with the knowledge of who they are, however, for many of us it is a continual learning process. Years ago, while at a Seminar on personal growth where I was challenged to really look at the dragons in the dark recesses of my memory, I saw a woman wearing a tee-shirt. On the front of the shirt there was a stage at the top and then all down the front of the shirt, was row after row of chairs. In the middle of this sea of chairs, was one person, all alone, looking toward the stage. Above the stage, was a

"I am afraid to show you who I really am, because if I show you who I really am, you might not like it--and that's all I got."

Sabrina Ward Harrison

sign that read, "1st Annual Convention of Children from Functional Families." Given some of the statistics available today, we begin to see that maybe dysfunctionality is normal. According to some surveys, more than 60% of children are from divorced families, and 72% of families are harboring someone with an addiction problem. Overall, I have heard estimates that over 90% of families are considered to be dysfunctional. So given all of this, I ask again, Who are you? Who are you beyond the perceptions of others and who THEY think you are.

Goleman says that, "People who have a high degree of self-awareness recognize how their feelings affect them, other people, and their job performance." He also states, that, "Someone who is highly self-aware knows where she is headed and why." Self-aware people have a strong sense of self! When we come to terms with those areas in our life that we are afraid to look at and recognize that they are simply areas to grow and learn, and not something that inherently bad or unfixable, we become much more comfortable with our shortcomings and are open to talking about them and even learn to use our own shortcomings as a way of connecting with others.

Self-Regulation

We all have emotions and sometimes it seems that our emotions take over, and often we are not quite sure why. Goleman likens self-regulation to that on-going inner conversation that we have and it frees us from being prisoners or our own feelings. When we become more

"*We are constantly being told what other people think we are, and that's why it is so important to know yourself.*"
Sarah McLachlan

self-aware, it becomes easier to regulate our emotions and not act on impulse. Viktor Frankl, survivor of the holocaust, writer, and someone who seems to possess tremendous self-regulation, said *"Between stimulus and response there is a space. In that space lies our freedom and our power to choose our response. In those choices lie our growth and our happiness."* Those who exhibit a great degree of self-regulation use that space between stimulus and response to determine the best response for the situation. Goleman writes that "…people who are in control of their feelings and impulses – that is, people who are reasonable – are able to create an environment of trust and fairness. In such an environment, politics and infighting are sharply reduced and productivity is high."

Motivation

Since the Hawthorne studies in the 1920's and '30's at the Western Electric plant near Chicago, IL first discovered that employees were motivated by factors other than economic gain as theorized by Frederick Taylor, the father of Scientific Management, the field of human motivation has been far reaching and had had a tremendous impact on organizations and how to best motivate employees. In terms of EI, Goleman found that motivation is the one trait that virtually all effective leaders have. He adds, "They are driven to achieve beyond the expectations – their own and everyone else's. The key word here is 'achieve.'" We are all motivated by a variety of things, however when we develop a deep "need" to achieve and work primarily for the ability to achieve more, we drive to achieve seems to be somewhat

"Only in growth, reform, and change, paradoxically enough, is true security to be found."
Anne Morrow Lindbergh

infectious and others follow suit. Those who tend to set the bar high for themselves, also tend to set it high for their organization, attracting others who want to achieve.

Empathy

I have already written my thoughts on Empathy as a component of leadership but I want to offer some of Goleman's thoughts on the matter. He says, that "Empathy is particularly important today as a component of leadership for at least three reasons: the increasing use of teams; the rapid pace of globalization and the growing need to retain talent. As a team leader it is imperative to have the ability to empathize with each member of the team, understand their emotions and where they are coming from, otherwise you run the risk of discounting, turning-off and losing a valuable team member. In a multicultural environment misunder-standings can arise very easily. Empathy can help a great deal in communicating with someone from a different cultural by truly listening with our hearts as well as our ears to pick up on clues that suggest that the words being spoken do not match with emotion or non-verbals being exhibited.

As I have said before, today's leaders need to be coaches and mentors. Goleman states that, "Empathy plays a key role in retention of talent, particularly in today's information economy. Leaders have always need empathy to develop and keep good people, but today the stakes are higher. When good people leave, they take the company's knowledge with them." Through coaching

"The only disability in life is a bad attitude."

Scott Hamilton

and mentoring employees, the pay-off comes, not only in better performance but in higher retention.

Social Skill

Goleman says that social skill is not just friendliness but friendliness with a purpose. Having the ability to interact with others in an engaging manner, getting to know people and the skills and capabilities and who they are as individuals, leaders can build a network of others that can be called on when needed. Goleman says, "Socially skilled people may at times appear not to be working while at work. They seem to be idly schmoozing – chatting in the hallways with colleagues or joking around with people who are not even connected with their "real" jobs. What they are actually doing is making connections, building their network, building bonds and alliances, and encouraging others, all they while recognizing that at some point in the future these contacts may come in very handy. Since the role of a leader is to get things done through people, making connections and understanding people seems to be an extremely great first step!

Becoming more emotionally intelligent takes effort, focus, commitment, drive and determination, but like anything really necessary it is worth the journey! I have always found it interesting that when I ask the students in my classes, "Who is afraid of failing?" almost every hand in the room will go up. Are you afraid of failing? Why? Why is that so? Why do so many people seem to be so afraid of failing? And what does "failing" mean?

283

"Only by much searching and mining are gold and diamonds obtained, and man can find every truth connected with his being if he will dig deep into the mine of his soul."

James Allen

Falling short of a goal or not achieving perfection, do these mean we failed? If we do not even attempt to do something then we have failed! But to strive to do something different, more than, better than we have done before and not reach our target, haven't we at least moved further than we have? Remember the bank Vice-President who didn't want to talk about setting a vision of achieving a 50% increase in customer base? Would he have failed if he only achieved 35% growth? Not if his previous growth would have only been about 10-15%

After a short discussion of why people were afraid of failing, I would then ask "How many of you are afraid of succeeding?" A few hands would go up, some would have a quizzical look on their face and then after a short period of time, several more hands would go up. Why? What is it about succeeding that many find frightening? The responses to this question have been very interesting, and seem to go back to the baggage being carried. Most often I would hear, "Well if I was really successful then others would expect that out of me all of the time and I don't know if I can maintain that level of success!" Why do we tend to sell ourselves short before we even start? So many times, I have heard something about "not being good-enough" as a reason for both a fear of failing and a fear of succeeding. As leaders, our main focus should be building those who follow. We should be doing everything we can to helping others discover the incredible power, abilities and potential within themselves, building their self-esteem and empowering and encouraging them to take risks and reach higher than they ever have before.

"The longer I live, the more I realize the impact of attitude on life. Attitude, to me, is more important than facts. It is more important than the past, the education, the money, than circumstances, than failure, than successes, than what other people think or say or do. It is more important than appearance, giftedness or skill. It will make or break a company... a church... a home. The remarkable thing is we have a choice everyday regarding the attitude we will embrace for that day. We cannot change our past... we cannot change the fact that people will act in a certain way. We cannot change the inevitable. The only thing we can do is play on the one string we have, and that is our attitude. I am convinced that life is 10% what happens to me and 90% of how I react to it. And so it is with you... we are in charge of our Attitudes."

Charles R. Swindoll

So, I ask you one more time, who are you? Where do you sell yourself short? What are you afraid of, fear or success, or both? How often do YOU tell yourself something that is negative in nature about what you are capable of doing? I mentioned earlier about growing up with the feeling of not being good enough, and that is the single most often heard statement I have heard from others! I find it amazing at how many people have a deep sense of not being capable, good enough, or not being worthy. What if, as a leader, you focused on continually building people up and helping them to see the better part of themselves? What if you spent your time letting those who follow you know that you truly believe in them and their capabilities? What has been so surprising to me, is seeing someone who "appears" to have it all, ability, talent, drive, ambition, etc., and then find that they have the same fears, self-doubt, and hesitancy to move due to a feeling of not being "good enough!"

The talent, potential and drive that is going untapped in every organization due to the fact that we spend so much time thinking about what we can't do rather than what is possible would be staggering if we could find a way to measure it! YOU are the leader that can make great changes in your organization, provided you discover the truth of who you really are and believe in yourself enough to truly believe in others! And then to help them believe in themselves! The choice is yours. When you decide to confront your deepest fears, look in the darkest recesses of your memories and look at all of the negative messages you tell yourself and get rid of the ones that

"Whereas the average individuals "often have not the slightest idea of what they are, of what they want, of what their own opinions are," self-actualizing individuals have "superior awareness of their own impulses, desires, opinions, and subjective reactions in general."

Abraham Maslow

simply are not true, you will truly become a STAR Leader!

"You never know yourself until you face the truth."
Pearl Bailey

CHAPTER NINE

Coach-ability

a: a private tutor b: one who instructs or trains; 1 a: the quality or state of being able *especially* : physical, mental, or legal power to perform **b:** competence in doing : skill2: natural aptitude or acquired proficiency

A Leader who is unable to coach, or to be coached by others, is lost in his or her own world and unable to grow!

A major part of being a leader in the 21st century is being a coach and a mentor. Question: Would you rather work for someone who is more than willing to tell you where you faults lay, someone who is quick to yell when he or she does not get their way? Or would you rather work for someone who recognizes that making a mistake is part of learning and growing both individually and as an organization? Someone who leads you to being a better person or all you can be by asking the right questions? Someone who seeks your advice also on how they themselves can be a better person, a better leader, a better coach?

Many years ago I heard a story, whether it is true or not I do not know for sure, but it makes an excellent point here:

"The goal of coaching is the goal of good management: to make the most of an organization's valuable resources."
HARVARD BUSINESS REVIEW

Supposedly, there was a manager for Southwestern Bell Telephone, when that company was still in existence, who made a huge mistake. The decision he made cost the company $6,000,000! An immediate loss on the bottom line! The next day, he was called into his boss's office. When he arrived, his boss said, "Well, I guess you know why I wanted to see you," to which the manager responded, "Yes I certainly do, you're going to fire me!" "Fire you?" his boss replied, "Why in the world would I fire you, I just spent $6,000,000 to train you! Why I want to talk to you is to look at what you would do differently next time, and to explore what you learned from this experience?"

Wow, who doesn't want to work for someone with that attitude? Where did we get the idea that we always have do something perfectly or we are going to be in trouble? I think it is due in large part because of the past autocratic management system that had little or no tolerance for mistakes! One aspect of our past approach to management was a very paternalistic style that required obedience and correct behavior.

If employees are not allowed to feel safe in making a mistake and that there is an all pervading feeling of, "if you screw up around here you are going to be fired, then how in the world are they going to be genuinely open to trying something new, to really work to make a difference in the organization? When employees work with a consistent sense of fear, they naturally will wait to be told what to do and not often be willing to try to solve

"The growth and development of people is the highest calling of leadership."

Harvey S. Firestone

a problem on their own or to try a new way of doing things. "It's not my job!" seems to be a resounding echo in many organizations.

There is a huge difference in making an honest mistake and doing something intentionally and intentional behavior is sabotage and should be dealt with swiftly and directly! In today's business environment, we need every employee, at every level, fully engaged and willing to work for the betterment of the organization without fear of being second guessed. Going forward in the 21st century, we need every employee to be engaged with their hearts, minds and souls, as well as their hands! Mistakes will happen! They happen all of the time. What we need are leaders who are able to coach employees to better performance, to look beyond the mistake itself and use it as an educating moment for better performance later. Learning to be a coach takes time, patience, understanding, empathy, and self-awareness!

Defining Moments

We all have moments in our lives when something happens and we sense a change in our lives. Certainly, a defining moment may be something truly major and significant that has happened, or maybe a defining moment can be something as simple as a coach's encouraging words at a particularly difficult time, or a leader's empathy and understanding when we truly make a mistake on the job. After all, don't we generally all feel pretty bad when we've made a mistake? We

"Lead and inspire people. Don't try to manage and manipulate people. Inventories can be managed but people must be led."
Ross Perot

certainly don't need someone else heaping condemnation on us at that moment because we are usually doing enough of that ourselves! A defining moment could be a kind word and a sympathetic ear! The real interesting thing about the events that happen in our lives is that we do not have control over WHAT happens, but we have total control over HOW we respond to those events!

Being a true coach means that you are willing to be authentic and open to the truth of who you are and focus entirely on the needs of the other person. It means that you are willing to put your judgments aside and focus entirely on encouraging and lifting the spirit of the person you are coaching and helping them see, for themselves without being told, where and how they can improve their performance and grow, learn and become a better person.

One thing a coach does not do is 'should' on people! Stop "shoulding" on others and for heaven sakes, stop "shoulding" on yourself! Whenever we use the word should, we immediately are telling the other person, or ourselves, that we aren't good enough because we have not done something right. Should is a judgment and judgments are not appropriate when coaching others! By asking the right open-ended questions a coach can lead the person being coached to a better understanding of how things can be done differently! Focus on the horizon of what is possible instead of what is wrong and help the person you are coaching to see their true potential.

"I know you've heard it a thousand times before. But it's true--hard work pays off. If you want to be good, you have to practice, practice, practice. If you don't love something, then don't do it."
Ray Bradbury

have allowed them to control your response! And that is a tremendous of power to give to someone else. A large part of being able to coach others, as well as having the ability and willingness to be coached, has to do with your attitude. Your attitude as a leader is fundamentally critical as it will impact the attitude and willingness to work for you of everyone around you!

Of course, we are each responsible for our own attitude, however, understanding this can sometimes be a bit difficult. No one, not one single person can put you in a bad mood unless you choose to be in a bad mood. You decide whether or not you are going to react to what someone else says or does and not them. Previously I talked about baggage and its impact on how we respond, and many times we let our baggage decide how we are going to respond. Being emotionally intelligent means

Attitude

Who is responsible for your attitude? You are, you say? Are you sure about that? Have you ever said, "He or she makes me so mad?" If you have, then you are saying that that other person is in control of your attitude! What you are saying is that in that instance you have given up your control of your own attitude to the other person and that we recognize the impact of our baggage and we take control of the situation and decide how we will respond.

This fact was pointed out very clearly to me early on in my life and this awareness has had a major impact on the way I see the world around me and how I respond to

"If you're not making mistakes, then you're not doing anything. I'm positive that a doer makes mistakes."

John Wooden

events that occur in my life. Shortly after high-school I began working for an electric utility. The CEO at the time was a retired judge who had phenomenal people skills. I still remember how he would stop in the hallway and talk to someone, asking how their day was going, chatting for a while about what was going on in their lives and then moving on. He had wonderful people skills and was very well liked by everyone in the company. He treated everyone with respect, kindness and truly listened.

In the early 1970's he retired and the new CEO was totally different. He was much more focused on financial matters and far less focused on the human side of the organization. Also, shortly after he became CEO, the company decided to build its first nuclear power plant. Given the aggressive activist nature of the 70's, this was an overwhelmingly daunting task. Also, due to the extremely expensive nature of building a nuclear plant, the vast majority of internal resources were focused on the construction of the plant, which left little for employee raises. The attitude of the employees of the company, not to mention the accompanying morale, went downhill faster than an avalanche. The company experienced a series of lengthy strikes, employees were surly and difficult to get along with and at the very low point, there were employees who were out going door-to-door to help get an initiative on the ballot to halt construction of the nuclear plant which essentially, would have put company in bankruptcy. It is totally unimaginable today that a company's employees would actively work to see the company go bankrupt, but that

"If you deliberately plan on being less than you are capable of being, then I warn you that you'll be unhappy for the rest of your life."
Abraham Maslow

was what was happening. When the senior management saw what was happening, they knew they had to do something to turn the tide. A consulting psychologist was brought in and he held a series of meetings with several hundred employees at a time. The focus of the meetings was to talk about attitude, personal responsibility and moving forward in a new direction. I was in my early 20's at the time and I must say, my attitude was probably close to being the worst of the lot. He told us how we have the power to choose how we see the world around us and that anytime we choose to let others determine our attitude then we are giving up far more than we are gaining. He also talked about how many people go through life blaming others for where they are in life, or who they are in life. Boy, did that hit home!

When he started saying this, my ears picked up and I really began to listen, because I felt that he was speaking about me specifically. As I mentioned earlier, I grew up with a father who had many issues of his own and was dragging around a great deal of psychological baggage. The primary message left me feeling lost in a sea of self-pity and an inability to see a better way. As I listened to this psychologist talk about family relationships and their impact on us a glimmer of a light began to shine. I distinctly remember him telling this room full of people, "If you want to blame your parents, teachers, or others in your life for where you are in life or for not allowing you to be who you think you should be, then fine. Blame them! Tell them, 'Shame on you for not being there for me! Shame on you for treating me the way you did' But

"Who exactly seeks out a coach? Winners who want even more out of life."
Chicago Tribune

if you are not any further along tomorrow to where you want to be, or any closer to being the person you want to be, then you had better look in the mirror and say 'Shame on you!' Wow, no one had ever said something like that to me before. There was so much I wanted to do and be and now I felt the full I could no longer blame my father and that the brunt of the responsibility for doing something about it was on my shoulders! In that moment, I saw that there was a way forward. He went on to tell everyone in the room that if we were really unhappy about where we are in life, including where we worked, then it was our responsibility to do something about. Incredible, he was telling us that it was up to us to go someplace else to work if we truly didn't like where we worked! He said, "Life is too short to spend it working for a company where you are miserable. You do NOT have to work here. Go find a company where you will be happy."

That may not sound so earth shattering today, but back then it was monumental to several people in the room, including me! One man stood up, and said, "That's not really true. I have to work here, I do not have a choice!" The consultant asked him if he had chains around his ankles that prevented him from leaving, to which he responded," You don't understand, I have a new house to pay for, as well as two kids in college, and that isn't cheap. So don't stand there and tell me I can go somewhere else to work because I can't! I have to work here!" The consultant looked at him and told him, "I hear that you have a new house to pay for and two kids in college, but what I want you to realize is, that those are

"Executives and HR managers know coaching is the most potent tool for inducing lasting personal change."
Ivy Business Journal

choices you are making, as well as working here is a choice. You are choosing to work here so that you can afford a new house and you can afford to pay for your children's education which is very commendable. If you do not want to work here to the point that you come to work angry and upset, then it may be time to make some different choices in your life! Maybe if you sold your house and bought a cheaper one or if you let your children pay for their own education you could afford to work somewhere else. But you are choosing to work here in order to do the things you want." The employee started to say that the consultant was wrong and then stopped in mid sentence as the impact of what he heard sank in and he slowly sat down as the words began to take hold for him.

Attitude – a personal responsibility! What a concept! I am responsible for the way I see the world around me and for what happens in my life! That was a totally new concept for me, and based on my interactions with others, there are many other people who even today do not understand that concept.

As a leader it is your responsibility to set the tone in your organization. I am a firm believer that 'What you give is what you get!' To further illustrate this point, I offer the following story. Anyone who has an email account I am sure, knows full well about those emails you get sent to you from well-meaning friends who feel that they have to forward everything they receive, especially if the message is one that promises untold riches or a plague of rats if it is not forwarded within the next few seconds.

"Part therapist, part consultant, part motivational expert, part professional organizer, part friend, part nag -- the personal coach seeks to do for your life what a personal trainer does for your body."

Minneapolis-St. Paul Star-Tribune

I'm often amazed at some of the messages I receive by rather intelligent people who say, "I normally don't believe in this but others say it works so I figured I don't have anything to lose so here it is. I typically delete all of these messages and very rarely forward anything unless it is something I thoroughly enjoyed or thought was of some value and then it is only to a select few friends. Shortly after I got an email account, in the mid-nineties, I received just such a message and I really enjoyed it. So much so that I saved it and I have read in just about every class I have facilitated since that time. I have often heard former students tell me that they were so taken by this story that they saved it and often read it and that it had made a tremendous difference in their life and how they chose to be a part of life instead of just reacting to it.

Attitude is Everything

By Francie Baltazar-Schwartz

Jerry was the kind of guy you love to hate. He was always in a good mood and always had something positive to say. When someone would ask him how he was doing, he would reply, "If I were any better, I would be twins." He was a unique manager because he had several waiters who had followed him around from restaurant to restaurant. The reason the waiters followed Jerry was because of his attitude. He was a natural motivator. If an employee was having a bad day, Jerry was there telling the employees how to look on the positive side of the situation. Seeing this style really

"What's really driving the boom in coaching, is this: as we move from 30 miles an hour to 70 to 120 to 180......as we go from driving straight down the road to making right turns and left turns to abandoning cars and getting motorcycles...the whole game changes, and a lot of people are trying to keep up, learn how not to fall."

John Kotter, Professor of Leadership, Harvard Business School

made me curious, so one day I went up to Jerry and asked him, "I don't get it! You can't be a positive person all of the time. How do you do it?" Jerry replied, "Each morning I wake up and say to myself, 'Jerry, you have two choices today. You can choose to be in a good mood or you can choose to be in a bad mood.' I choose to be in a good mood. Each time something bad happens, I can choose to be a victim or I can choose to learn from it. I choose to learn from it. Every time someone comes to me complaining, I can choose to accept their complaining or I can point out the positive side of life. I choose the positive side of life."

"Yeah, right, it's not that easy." I protested.

"Yes it is," Jerry said. "Life is all about choices. When you cut away all the junk, every situation is a choice. You choose how you react to situations. You choose how people will affect your mood. You choose to be in a good mood or bad mood. The bottom line: It's your choice how you live life."

I reflected on what Jerry said. Soon thereafter, I left the restaurant industry to start my own business. We lost touch, but I often thought about him when I made a choice about life instead of reacting to it.

Several years later, I heard that Jerry did something you are never supposed to do in a restaurant business: he left the back door open one morning and was held up at gunpoint by three armed robbers. While trying to open the safe, his hand, shaking from nervousness, slipped off

"I never cease to be amazed at the power of the coaching process to draw out the skills or talent that was previously hidden within an individual, and which invariably finds a way to solve a problem previously thought unsolvable."

John Russell, Managing Director,
Harley-Davidson Europe Ltd.

. the combination. The robbers panicked and shot him.

Luckily, Jerry was found relatively quickly and rushed to the local trauma center. After 18 hours of surgery and weeks of intensive care, Jerry was released from the hospital with fragments of the bullets still in his body. I saw Jerry about six months after the accident. When I asked him how he was, he replied "If I were any better, I'd be twins. Wanna see my scars?"

I declined to see his wounds but did ask him what had gone through his mind as the robbery took place. "The first thing that went through my mind was that I should have locked the back door," Jerry replied. "Then, as I lay on the floor, I remembered that I had two choices: I could choose to live, or I could choose to die. I chose to live."

"Weren't you scared? Did you lose consciousness?" I asked.

Jerry continued, "The paramedics were great. They kept telling me I was going to be fine. But when they wheeled me into the emergency room and I saw the expressions on the faces of the doctors and nurses, I got really scared. In their eyes, I read, 'He's a dead man.' I knew I needed to take action."

"What did you do?" I asked. "Well, there was a big burly nurse shouting questions at me," said Jerry. "She asked if I was allergic to anything. 'Yes,' I replied.

"Attitudes are contagious, are yours worth catching?"
Unknown

The doctors and nurses stopped working as they waited for my reply...I took a deep breath and yelled, 'Bullets!' Over their laughter, I told them, 'I am choosing to live. Operate on me as if I am alive, not dead."

Jerry lived thanks to the skill of his doctors but also because of his amazing attitude. I learned from him that every day we have the choice to live fully. Attitude, after all is everything!

Beyond Attitude

So how do we become better coaches? We first need to understand ourselves and why we feel it is important. Why do you want to be a coach? Do you really see the value in supporting others in a journey of personal growth and fulfillment? Do you really see the value in having employees who are focused on being the best they can be? Do you really want them to be willing to follow you on your quest to achieve your vision without having to be told what to do every single moment? Knowing and understanding these things is essential in coaching. You have to know, deep within yourself, why it is important. Understanding the differences in personalities and how people behave and communicate based on personality styles is essential in being a great coach. The 21st century leader at times needs to be psychologist, a sociologist, as well as many other 'ologists' and needs to be a student of culture and its impact on behavior. Today's leaders must fundamentally understand and believe that there are no bad employees, only employees who sometimes have bad behaviors. The fundamental

"Why is it so hard to lead yourself? The answer, in my experience, lies in the differences between your idealized self—how you see yourself and how you want to be seen—and your real self. The key to growing as a leader is to narrow that gap by developing a deep self-awareness that comes from straight feedback and honest exploration of yourself, followed by a concerted effort to make changes."

Bill George

Quoted in Fast Company

aspect is that the 21st century leader must be emotionally intelligent and focused on her followers rather than on herself, her wants and her needs. Only through truly putting others first do we gain beyond measure and achieve the things we truly want.

There are many great books on coaching and acquiring great facilitation skills, as well as a host of consultants and training facilitators who would love to help you learn. But you cannot simply rely on books or consultants to make you a better coach or a better leader! You have to have the "want to." You have to feel the fire in your gut that will drive you forward. You have to be willing to learn first-hand by doing, by being willing to make a mistake and to be willing to seek out the advice of those around you. Find someone who you feel does a great job at coaching and ask them to coach you. Also be open to feedback from those above you, beside you and those who are following you. Being a great coach or a great leader is no different than learning to play a musical instrument really well or being able to play tennis, golf or other sport really well. It takes training, practice, practice and more practice!

Find someone you believe to be a good personal coach and ask them how they do it. Ask them to be your mentor, someone with whom you can talk to about your successes, your missteps, your fears, and your vision. You must also be willing to be coached by those you are leading and open to their feedback, after all, they are the ones you want to be a coach for, right? Opening yourself to the truth of how others see you and what they really

317

"I certainly don't regret my experiences because without them, I couldn't imagine who or where I would be today. Life is an amazing gift to those who have overcome great obstacles, and attitude is everything!"

Sasha Azevedo

want and need from you can be a bit scary to many people but it is absolutely essential.

One of the best tools available, that is not utilized near often enough, is the 369 degree feedback system. Many organizations still rely on the performance evaluation as the mainstay of letting employees know how they are doing. Although the performance evaluation can be a great tool, if used correctly as a coaching tool, I find that so many organizations still use it as a way for the boss to tell an employee where they really messed up during the last year! I often ask those in my classes who receives or gives performance evaluations and practically every hand will go up. I then ask "Who likes to give or receive a performance evaluation?" and almost every hand in the room would go down. Occasionally, someone would say they really like to get a performance evaluation because it is important to them to know how they are doing and where they can improve. If used correctly, a performance review can be very useful, however, like I said, it seems that so very few organizations use it correctly.

In many cases I have seen, performance evaluations are seen as more of a nuisance, something to endure or an opportunity for the boss to go off on the employee and bring up all the things that were done "wrong" in the past year. Is there any wonder why many people view the performance in a negative light? I once shared the services of a secretary, as the position was called back then, with the Vice-President to whom I reported. Dee was a extraordinarily great example of a personal

"Weakness of attitude becomes weakness of character."

Albert Einstein

assistant before that term became the norm for someone in her job. She was exceptional at anticipating needs, getting things done before they were needed and was always positive and helpful. One day as I returned to the office from the field, Dee was coming out of the VP's office in tears. I asked, "Dee what is wrong, are you okay?" She responded by saying that she couldn't talk about it and left quickly. She later came to my office and told me that when I saw her she had just received her performance evaluation and that she had been rated down because one time during the previous year she had failed to fill the boss' paper clip cup! One extremely minor slip and she was rated lower than she should have been! The boss was one that believed that the performance evaluation was a time to tell the employee what they did wrong, instead of mentioning it at the time of the incident. Some time back I was going to be speaking to a group of Federal employees about the use of performance appraisals and I so I did a search on the internet for any information that might be relevant and I found a site that listed actual comments found on performance evaluations of Federal employees:

- *His men would follow him anywhere, but only out of morbid curiosity!*
- *He would be out of his element in a parking lot puddle.*
- *When she opens her mouth it is only to change feet.*
- *He consistently sets low standards of achievement and continually fails to meet them.*
- *He is depriving a village somewhere of an idiot*

"Your living is determined not so much by what life brings to you as by the attitude you bring to life; not so much by what happens to you as by the way your mind looks at what happens."

Kahlil Gibran

- *If he were any more stupid he would need to be watered twice a week.*

WOW! If employees are truly this bad, then why are they still employed? I cannot imagine anyone wanting to work in environment where the people who wrote these comments played any role in supervising or managing people! There is absolutely no reason whatsoever for people like this to be in a leadership position and the fact that they are says a great deal about those at the top of the organization! Not long ago, I was facilitating a class on leadership for a group of Federal employees in Cleveland, OH and read these comments. Later during a break, one of the participants came to me and he asked for my email address as he had a couple of articles written about toxic leadership. When I received the articles I found them to be very interesting. Toxic leaders are those who yell, demand, bluster, threaten, and intimidate in order to get the things done they want done. They do not think anything about those whom they are leading other than they are tools to be used and discarded when needed. The articles talked about the fact toxic leaders need to be identified early and removed the organization. The author recognized that fact that toxic leaders do get things done and are often sent into an area where immediate action is needed and when they accomplish what is needed they are rewarded by being promoted or sent to another assignment to get immediate accomplishment of another task. The problem with toxic leaders, the author recognized, is not whether or not they are able to get things done, but the wake of destruction in morale and enthusiasm they leave behind. The author

"The difference between what we do and what we are capable of doing would suffice to solve most of the world's problems."

Mahatma Gandhi

stated that often some of the best and brightest of the young people leave the organization because they do not want to be a part of that type of environment! Maybe a toxic leader in the past could get away with that type of behavior because not many people were willing to change jobs and would simply put up with it. Today, however, those who are known as Milennials are not willing to tolerate behavior like that and see nothing wrong with simply walking out the door and not coming back.

Although I did not walk off the job, I did not stay longer than was absolutely necessary when I experienced a toxic leader. Many years ago, I was in the Air National Guard and after my six year tour was up, I would have liked to have stayed but was unwilling due to the leadership I experienced. During my exit interview I was asked if there was a reason I was not willing to re-up and I said absolutely, I told the interviewer that it was because of the commander of the unit I was in. He was a known alcoholic, and was a bully and someone who had no business being in a command position. The interviewer responded by saying that he had heard it before but there was nothing he could do about it!

"If we do not have performance evaluations, then how do we ever let people know how they are doing?" This is a question I have heard often. As I mentioned earlier, the360 degree feedback process, I believe, is an absolute must for everyone in the organization, especially for leaders! With a 360 degree feedback evaluation, the person being reviewed first fills out the same evaluation

"One can never consent to creep when one feels the compulsion to soar!"

Helen Keller

as everyone else. Then the form is sent to his or her superior, a selected number of peers, as well as a selected number of direct reports. It is always interesting to see how someone rated themselves and then compare that to how the other groups rated him or her. An important element of this process is that it is strictly anonymous. There are only two people from whom the responses are known to the person being evaluated: herself and her supervisor. All responses are sent to an independent third party who acts as a facilitator and who puts together a report, which they go over with the person being evaluated. This way, peers and direct reports are free to give open and honest feedback.

A few years ago, I was in Connecticut conducting a 360 review feedback session for a division manager. One of the questions on the evaluation read, "How well does this individual keep his/her direct reports updated and informed on what is going on in the company?" Well, as we began talking about this question, he was very proud of his ability to communicate with his employees. In fact, on a scale of 1-10 with 10 being the best, he rated himself a '9,' his boss rated him '10' and his peers rated him '9's' and '10's." When we looked at how his direct reports rated him, things fell apart! He had asked that all eight of his direct reports rate him as he was really interested in what everyone had to say. On this particular question, 4 out of 8 of his employees rated him '9-10' and the other four each rated him '2!' He was totally shocked and speechless when he saw this. "What's going on here?" I asked him. "I don't have a clue!" he

"The most exciting breakthroughs of the 21st century will not occur because of technology but because of an expanding concept of what it means to be human"

John Naisbitt

said in total bewilderment. "I feel like I make a real effort to keep everyone informed, this really floors me!" We talked about possibilities with no enlightenment so we went on to the next question. Half way through our discussion of the next question his face totally lit up and I knew he had the answer. "What is it?" I asked. "I know exactly what is going on," he said. "Half of the people who report to me sit right outside my office and I am always out there talking to them about what's happening and the latest info, and half the my people sit on the opposite side of the building and I never go over there!" "Very interesting," I said, "What are you going to do about that?" "Well, the first thing I'm going to do as soon as we are finished here is go over to where they are and I am making a point of going over there every day!" He said with a look of amazed awareness.

If, as leaders, we are not open to feedback from others, including and especially those whom we are leading, how do we ever know when there is something that is being mis-communicated or misunderstood? Leaders need to work in building their empathy and understanding of others. Leaders also need to improve on their ability to be a coach and mentor instead of a director and a dictator. Leaders also need to constantly seek out feedback from others. You need to continually evaluate if you are becoming the leader you want to be. The choice is yours! You are, at any given moment, the person you have chosen to be! The choices you have made have led you to this point in your life and have determined how you lead. If you want to be a better leader, then make the choice and be willing to open

"You cannot control what happens to you, but you can control your attitude toward what happens to you, and in that, you will be mastering change rather than allowing it to master you."

Brian Tracy

yourself up to the feedback from others, as scary as it might be!

I understand that there are those in the Human Resources arena who will argue that a 360 degree review has a different objective than a performance evaluation. They argue the 360 is solely for development and there is no ability to offer merit rewards based solely on a 360 degree evaluation. There may be an element of truth to this, however I have not seen a performance evaluation system that provides much in the way of benefits to the organization or to the individual being rated. Once a 360 review is completed, the next step should be that the leader and the employee should work jointly, with the leader coaching the employee in establishing very clear performance goals for the following year. At the end of the goal year, the employee would most likely be the first one to determine whether or not the goals were attained. This is the best way to instill ownership of one's own performance, as opposed to a "parent figure" complimenting or admonishing for goals attained or missed. Another criticism of a 360 degree evaluation system is its cost. Yes, it does some additional costs in having an independent facilitator process the responses and provide a feedback session to the person being evaluated. And it also involves extra time by those filling out the evaluations, but the question I have, is what do you want? Do you want employees who are waiting to have a bomb dropped on them or employees who are focused on self-improvement and looking forward to getting feedback from a variety of sources on areas they are doing well or maybe areas where they

"Without a healthy dose of heart, a supposed "leader" may manage, but he does not lead."

Daniel Goleman, Richard Boyatzis &
Annie Mckee
"Primal Leadership'"

could improve? Organizations will spend a great deal on making the outside of their business look good and then balk at spending money on helping their employees look good!

"The key to successful leadership today is influence, not authority."
Ken Blanchard

CHAPTER TEN
BE A *STAR* LEADER

A Leader who has Vision and Passion and leads with a focus of Integrity while Communicating in an Emotionally Intelligent way with Empathy, and self-Knowledge and has the ability to Coach and be Coached and can put it all together, can accomplish amazing things through the power of intention and the sheer magic of the people who are willing to follow him or her!

Well, I am assuming that if you have made it this far you most likely have a genuine interest in leadership. I don't know however, whether or not that interest is simply in the subject of leadership itself or whether you truly are interested in being a STAR leader of the future. It is very easy to say that "Yes, I want to be a great leader. I want to be a STAR leader!" However, words are cheap. Action is where the proof lies! Being a great leader is much like being a great musician. You don't learn how to play a musical instrument by reading a book. You don't learn to play an instrument by listening to someone tell you how to do it. Learning to play comes by picking up the instrument, playing some pretty awful notes, practicing, studying, learning and growing over a period of time. However, when it comes to leadership it seems that many people think that if they read enough books, or see enough good and bad leaders, they can learn to become a truly great leader. Being a great leader comes from doing, making mistakes, being open to learn from

"If you can find a path with no obstacles, it probably doesn't lead anywhere."
Frank A. Clark

those mistakes, receiving feedback from others, involving others, and going on. True leadership does not mean that you are better than everyone else, or even looking like you are better than everyone else. True leadership is letting yourself be seen as an average human being, just like your followers, but an average human being with a vision and deep passion!

Vision: To be a true STAR Leader, you have to know where you are going. You have to know, very specifically, what it is you want to achieve. You have to allow yourself the opportunity to dream and to look at what is possible. You must be bold in your vision! Your dreams and your vision need to be challenging, for if they are not, they will not stir the interest and enthusiasm of those who are waiting to be led to greater heights. Fear, seems to be the number one deterrent to a clear vision. Fear of failing, as well as, a fear of succeeding. Nothing great has ever been achieved by wanting to "keep doing as well as we have."

Integrity: Along with a clear, strong, challenging vision, we have to maintain integrity to that vision with the full tenacity of a charging lion chasing prey. The prey of the organization is the vision, and if you're hungry, then absolutely nothing should stand in your way or detract your focus. Every member of your organization should feel the same way, and should be willing to go to great lengths to capture the elusive prey of your vision. Everyone should feel the "fire in the belly" for achieving the vision, and that comes from the leader's constant focus on why it is important, why the vision

"The task of the leader is to get his people from where they are to where they have not been."

Henry Kissinger

must be achieved. The mere act of rewarding an individual or department for doing something not directed at achieving the vision, will tell everyone that the vision is not important.

Passion: What things have you accomplished in your life for which you had no passion? What things have you done, on your own, for which you truly did not care whether you did them or not? Nothing, right? While Vision is the fuel that drives the organization to success, Passion is the spark that ignites the fuel! Remember, above all else, if you do not really care about achieving the vision, no one else is going to give it one bit of interest. If you see achieving the vision as a chore, and obligation, a job that simply has to be done and one that you are not deeply passionate about, you will be finished before you begin!

Empathy: Putting yourself in the skin of someone else and seeing things through their eyes allows you as a leader to truly understand the organization, to understand your follows, and to understand what is needed in your quest to achieve the vision. Recognizing that each and every employee of your organization has feelings, emotions, baggage, hopes, desires, and has a deep innate need to achieve with a growing desire to be a part of something greater than themselves will allow you, the leader, to inspire them to bring out the greater part of themselves. Not in order to achieve the vision, but just because you deeply care about helping them achieve their own greatness! Of course, a by-product is, every-one will do anything they possibly can to achieve the

"People are more easily led than driven."
David Harold Fink

vision because they truly feel you care about them, you are deeply passionate about achieving the vision and about helping them to be all they can be.

Knowledge: Who are you? Knowing who you are, what makes you tick, why you do the things you do, what motivates you, what you deeply care about, what your values are, what your personality types is and how it impacts how you communicate with others and where you want to go or what you want to achieve is paramount in your role as a leader. If you do not know these things, or at least work every day to learn these things, I believe you will continually encounter major roadblocks in your journey to being a STAR leader. STAR Leaders of the 21st century will be constant learners, avidly seeking knowledge from many sources, especially about self! Knowledge of your True Self, will undoubtedly give you a sense of calm, acceptance and self-love that will allow you to accept the bruises and headaches, temporary set-backs and failures that you will encounter in working to achieve your vision that you are so passionate about.

Communication: Knowing where you are going, aligning the entire organization in that direction, deeply caring about where you are going, being empathetic and having all of the knowledge in the world are not going to help you if you are unable to communicate clearly, directly and with conviction! Communicating where you are going, and why, must be done every single day, every hour of every day, and every minute of every hour! It is communicated not only in the words you use, but most importantly, in the things you do. STAR Leaders

"Leadership should be born out of the understanding of the needs of those who would be affected by it."

Marian Anderson

recognize that followers need to be constantly reassured that the vision is attainable and that they have the capacity to achieve something greater than themselves. Communicate in ways that inspire the hearts of your followers and your role as a STAR Leader will be infinitely easier!

Emotional Intelligence: Recognizing the fact that you are an emotional being, as wells as recognizing that your followers are also emotional beings is foremost in your understanding of emotional intelligence. Recognizing the baggage you carry with you every day, as well as its impact on your behavior and how you interact with others is vitally important to your success, even more so, than your mental intelligence, according to Daniel Golman. Becoming more emotionally intelligent will open a great number of doors for you that you might have found closed before. I have seen this first hand and deeply understand how being emotionally unintelligent can have a negative impact.

I am not usually a regular listener of National Public Radio. However, recently, on one of the shows, a guest was talking about "baggage" and how baggage is a major player in our role of a leader. This gentleman used a rather interesting analogy about how we all have baggage and we can help each other reach our goal by recognizing that we are not alone. The analogy he used was *The Wizard of Oz!* He described how Dorothy was a young girl who was in a place where she was completely alone, had no idea where she was going, but she had a very clear idea of what she wanted. I think the underlying

"Nearly all men can stand adversity, but if you want to test a man's character, give him power."
Abraham Lincoln

messages in stories like *The Wizard of Oz* are what draw us to them and help them earn a place in our collective consciousness. I mean, who has not seen *The Wizard of Oz*?

Who has not watched this movie without feeling some deeper tug at your heart or sub-consciousness with a sense of deep longing of your own for something more? Listening to this guest talk about Dorothy and her friends made me think about how this applied to Leadership and I saw a very clear comparison. Dorothy had a very clear vision of what she wanted. She knew where she wanted to go, and she knew that it was not going to be easy, however she was willing to do whatever was necessary in order to "go home." Along the way, she met Scarecrow, Tin Man and the Cowardly Lion, all who had their own needs or vision of what they wanted and they all realized that through their mutual needs and wants they could help each other. In other words, they each had their own WII-FM, "what's in it for me", and through their efforts together they had a deep belief that they could get to Oz and realize their dreams.

Recognizing that, yes, we all have baggage can go a very long way in helping us in working together. By realizing this simple fact, I believe, we all will look at each other with a little bit more compassion, understanding and empathy. I'm not talking about having large pity parties where we all sit around and talk about how we weren't treated fairly when we were growing up. I'm talking about just the simple recognition that 1) we are not alone, and 2) the behaviors exhibited by others may be driven

"Leadership is understanding people and involving them to help you do a job. That takes all of the good characteristics, like integrity, dedication of purpose, selflessness, knowledge, skill, implacability, as well as determination not to accept failure."

Admiral Arleigh A. Burke

by their baggage and if we made a little effort to confront that behavior on that recognition, we just might have a different outcome. We all need to work to "get over" our baggage!

Coach-ability: The ability to be a coach for those around you, as well as having the ability, the openness to being coached yourself draws others to you and opens their hearts and minds to what you want to achieve. No other ability is greater in inspiring the hearts of others. Few people will forget the impact a special person in their lives had on them when they felt that person had their best interest at heart. We all recognize the genuine caring and empathy someone else shows for who we are and where we are in our lives. Coaches truly stand out as those who mentor the heart. Be a coach and be open to allowing others to coach you and you will go a long way in becoming a STAR Leader!

Homework

If you truly want to become a STAR Leader, as I've mentioned several times, it takes constant work and self reflection. To begin with, keeping in mind the eight STAR qualities, Vision, Integrity, Passion, Empathy, Knowledge, Communication, Emotional Intelligence and Coach-ability, work through the STAR process, being completely honest with yourself. To do this, focus on:

S – Strengths
T – Traits

"A new leader has to be able to change an organization that is dreamless, soulless and visionless ... someone's got to make a wakeup call."
Warren Bennis

A – Attitude

R – Results

Strengths: Making a list of your all of your strengths that will assist you in becoming a STAR Leader. Work through each of the eight attributes, one at a time, and make a list of the strengths you possess that will help you become better in each area. This is not a time for modesty. Ask others what they see your strengths are. Question constantly. Take a hard look at yourself!

Talents: What talents do you possess in each area? Are you a natural visionary? Are you naturally focused on achieving what you start out to achieve? What parts of your personality will work for you as you strive to be more focused, a better communicator, more inspirational while remaining true to achieving your vision? Do you possess talents in sports, music or some other area? How might those talents translate to your role as leader? How might you learn from other areas of your life?

Attitude: What is your attitude toward becoming a STAR Leader? Do you see it as something that sounds good and you will "work toward being better?" Or do you have an attitude that this is extremely important and you are going to do everything you can to achieving great success as a leader? What is your attitude toward other people? Do you see everyone as being capable of doing great things, or do you see others more as a hindrance, a necessary evil to put up with on your journey through life?

"The best example of leadership is leadership by example."

Jerry McClain

Results: What are the results you want to achieve? What do they look like? If you achieved these results, how would you life, your organization, the world be different? For some, I know this may be difficult, based on personality type, for some have difficulty seeing what can be, without specific data to build up to what's possible, but continue to work on it. Be as detailed in your description as possible. What does being a STAR Leader of the 21st century look like to you? How would it be different from where or what you see yourself as now? Are you the person you want to be? What does your ideal self look like? If you were the absolute 'best' person you could be, what would it look like? Make a list of the traits or attributes of you "ideal self". What results do you want to see? This may take some time, but don't give up, when you have gone as far as you believe you can go, put it aside for a while and come back to it and work some more. The clearer the image you can see in your mind, the more focused you will become.

By focusing not only on your Strengths, Traits, Attitude and Results, but on the STAR characteristics of those you are leading, you become a leader that is focused on positive attributes. Spend time working through the STAR process for each person you lead. Get to know them, understand their strengths and look at how you can inspire them to greater ability. You will become a leader on the good things inherent in yourself and others and you will become a leader that is focused on constant improvement and achieving the best in yourself as well as the best in others!

"If your actions inspire others to dream more, learn more, do more and become more, you are a leader."

John Quincy Adams

Quotes: Throughout this book, I have included a great number of quotes about leadership, vision, communication, as well as other subjects. I love quotes for they often speak volumes in a relatively small number of words. I have collected quotes about leadership for quite some time and have used them in many of my leadership classes. I always found it interesting to hear those in my classes talk about what they learned from specific quotes, so I invite you to go back through this book again and read just the quotes, pausing to reflect on each one and what it means to you. What message do you get when you read a particular quote? Do you agree, disagree, and why? Does a particular quote stand out to you? If so, why? What do you believe your interest in this particular quote says about who you are as a leader? Self reflection is critical to personal growth and personal growth is essential in being a STAR Leader of the 21st century! I wish you the all the best on your leadership journey, and I will leave you with my favorite quote of all time:

"In one day, Samson slew 1,000 Philistines with the jawbone of an ass. Every day, scores of workers have their trust and commitment killed by the same weapon."

Unknown

www.ingramcontent.com/pod-product-compliance
Lightning Source LLC
Chambersburg PA
CBHW071356170526
45165CB00001B/62

*9 7 8 1 4 4 1 4 9 5 8 5 3 *